Cipher Method

Cipher Method

Cipher Method

An Operations Management, Supply Chain,
Lean, and HR Perspective

DAVIS R CONWAY

First Printing, 2019

KDP ISBN 9781095645642

First Edition

To my Wife for her unwavering support and tolerance.

To Dr. Joseph Martinich for opening my eyes to environmental sustainability.

To Professor John Earls for providing an aha moment.

Contents

Preface

Every mom believes their child is a genius, people who excel or make advances in their field are often called genius, and some people just call themselves a genius hoping to raise their perceived social status. Many people believe a high understanding of math or an ability to perform mathematical party tricks are a sign of genius, and several believe being a genius involves photographic or eidetic memory superpowers. None of this is factual, while eidetic memory seems to exist in children on rare occasion, it eventually dissipates and is probably not what you think it is in the first place. Photographic memory is a myth, primarily used to project superior intelligence in storylines for film and television. The truth is many intellectually gifted people are not even masters of basic arithmetic. Quick what is 378/7.4? No idea, give me some paper and a pencil or just use the damn calculator on your phone!

Virtually none, if any of us, are like the characters from the Big Bang Theory TV show. I am six foot two, or less now due to normal shrinkage, weigh 300 pounds (working on that), chew tobacco (working on that too), curse like a construction worker at times (I guess I am working on a lot of things), and like to fish, golf, shoot, and collect coins. I tend to drink to excess during social gatherings with my close friends and do crazy things or make an ass out of myself. In my younger days, I was a bouncer in a heavy metal bar and have been on both ends of a good brawl. My everyday appearance gives no indication of my economic or intellectual status.

A high IQ is a natural ability; it cannot be significantly increased through education or training. Education, with exception to theoretical studies and research, is merely the understanding of established process steps. Someone with a high IQ can be highly educated but being highly educated does not equate to a high IQ. Having a doctorate only indicates that someone successfully completed a predefined set of process steps that vary in quality and difficulty between issuing institutions. But neither the natural ability or the earned education is something to dismiss or automatically assume one or the other will make a better employee.

After a point in elementary school, my grades became lackluster, and in high school, I focused on what I needed to pass and obtain the required credits. It was not uncommon for me to have a failing grade at the quarter to be quickly raised to an acceptable letter grade of D with a couple of A assignments or tests belched out the second quarter of the semester. I was such a smartass in high school one teacher agreed to give me a D if I never returned to her class. We both lived up to our part of the deal. My senior year I nearly failed to graduate by ¼ credit in physical education because I never went to class. I had planned my final semester to allow plenty of time to hang out in the auto shop where we routinely socialized drinking alcohol instead of attending class. Fortunately, the PE teacher showed me some pity since the class was taken as an elective and awarded me my customary D.

I did not have the option to go to college after high school, my parents never promoted the idea and my grades did not warrant any scholarships. I obtained my BS late in life after the recent recession left me with a large amount of time on my hands. Back in my early twenties, I started to realize that there was something different about myself compared to others, so I registered to take the proctored testing offered by Mensa. My testing results not only qualified me for Mensa, they additionally qualified me for membership in Intertel.

Mensa is the international high IQ society that requires an IQ in the 98th percentile for membership and Intertel requires an IQ in the 99th percentile. To clarify, 98th percentile does not equate to 2 out of every 100 people. This percentile is based on the standard bell curve of all historically tested IQ's. Without going into explaining bell curves, you should understand that you may not randomly meet more than a handful of Mensa members in your lifetime. When you further calculate the probability of a person meeting someone in the 99th IQ percentile, outside of a convention or similar, it is most likely never. My brother tested into the same organizations a couple of years after I did and is the only other Intertel member I have met in 25 years. While Intertel membership has grown over the last couple of decades, there are only about 1,500 qualified members compared to Mensa's 134,000.

Unfortunately, having a high IQ does not equate to being imparted with the knowledge of the universe at birth, or subjects like math are as natural as breathing. What I do know is that my comprehending and study requirements were far less time consuming than my fellow college students, and problem-solving always results in people looking in my direction. While some material was what I considered challenging, graduating Magna Cum Laude was not. But never fear, having a high IQ does not mean you are never incorrect.

When I was accepted into Mensa, I immediately told my work supervisor because I looked up to him and consider him to have been one of my primary mentors in life to this day. He looked at me and asked, "So, what do you think that will do for you?" I replied, "Open many doors." I was profoundly incorrect.

I always become quite embarrassed when the subject comes up and eventually started to hide my intelligence status unless necessary. Unfortunately, this book requires some additional justification of competency outside of experience and entrepreneurial success. When you mention that you are a member of Mensa people usually doubt you, and when you produce your membership card 99% of them react opposite of the way you would imagine. People generally become defensive and behave like you are an adversary of some sort. People generally avoid asking you anything and either set out to prove you are not as smart as you think you are or unfairly set you to a higher standard than everyone else. This behavior includes demeaning and insulting comments or looks if your immediate answer is "I do not know" to any infinite possibilities of subject matter, some even resort to sabotage to ensure failure.

When you think about the prior probability of meeting a person certified in the 99th percentile of IQ and then figure in the probability of one of those people looking for work and being experienced in the field of study you are looking to hire, the probability becomes astronomically low. I decided to submit my resume to several advertised positions that were either in my field of expertise or closely related. I received ZERO follow-up inquiries to those applications.

The companies that replied to my inquiries about their selection process after the position was filled had the following to say:

- Their software did not select the application for further review.
- Their first round of selection is solely based on their questionnaire, and master's degrees are given preference.
- The CV or cover letter were never reviewed, and the qualifications were never seen.
- The qualifications seen in the cover letter were misunderstood or considered false, embellished, or perceived as arrogance and not a good cultural fit.
- While we advertised for entrepreneurial skills, people educated in the subject are given preference, but people with actual entrepreneurial experience are rejected due to the belief they would not be satisfied working for others.

This experiment resulted in a greater understanding of the ostracization of Albert Einstein by his academic peers and the reliance of a close friend to obtain a low-level job at the patent office to afford marriage. Why did Albert have such a hard time finding a job to provide even a basic income to support marriage? Employers poor understanding of potential, fear of internal competition, or maybe the inability to overlook social or behavior oddities? It is not a secret Albert was not what we would today call a good cultural fit, something that has always been difficult to overlook by the mainstream. Today, being a good cultural fit has been elevated to an importance greater than skill, potential, or profit.

If you call me, I will help reduce your cost and increase your production. But, I will most likely forget your name 10 seconds after you tell me, interrupt you mid-sentence, not hear a word you say (my wife's favorite) when I am focused, or possibly have my shirt on inside out. All things that I work very hard to correct because they can appear like I do not care, but this is not the case. You could offer me a million dollars to remember 15 people's names 10 minutes after you tell them to me and I would probably fail every time. Having a variation of my own name is not always an exception to the rule.

I am a certified genius on the top end of the genius scale, so what are you going to do? Work to prove me wrong? Or listen to a unique perspective and use it for your benefit? Actually, either choice serves the purpose outlined in this book.

Chapter 1

Leading Ourselves to Average

A business is an entity that needs to make a profit from the fickle, unpredictable, and infinitely variable thought processes of humans, commonly referred to as "the invisible hand." To achieve this goal business relies on the same wide-ranging variables of humans to operate. In other words, we are looking for the definitive answer to making a profit from chaos by using chaos to do it.

We are constantly searching for the answer to an impossible question; what are the process steps that guarantee a successful business? We take classes and read books telling us we must do this or that to be successful because it worked for them or someone they studied. We are bombarded with poorly translated Japanese terms or processes like Six Sigma promising to make everything we do the best it can be. We listen to savvy salespeople profoundly confident that their equipment or software will save or make us untold multiples of our current situation. We are naive when it comes to the flavor of the month, poorly studied hypothesis, success stories that can never truly be replicated, and misinterpretation of subject matter in the hopes it will fix all our problems and make us look like an innovative rock star.

It seems like every business book to date is about what someone else has done within a single unique environment, what a single unreplicated study has determined, the educated musings of Ph.D.'s who have never actually created a long term multiple employee successful business, or people who try to display a superior business acumen by using existing business techniques and claiming some profound revelation. This is not one of those books; those books are for the people who strive to be average through conformity.

You must come to terms with the fact no book, class, professor, mentor, or consultant will ever be able to provide empirical proof that following a specific set of process steps will always lead to business success. The best these people can do is provide hindsight from very specific, impossible to replicate, business scenarios. But hindsight provides insight into our own specific set of circumstances; the real question is what do you do with this information? Use it to improve or blindly replicate it hoping for a similar outcome?

This book is meant to be a guide, information that gives perspective allowing you to make the best choices for your unique situation. You will find that much of the book's information is given in very basic generalities, because like people, every business is different and giving one size fits all solutions would make this book no more effective than any other book. It is like writing a book about how to install tile in your bathroom. I can tell you how to cut, support, and attach every possible type of tile but there is a limit to the useful

2

information I can give you without looking at your specific project and knowing what tile color, pattern, size, shape, or finish you like. You must do the work and make the final decisions yourself.

You may learn a new perspective from this book or just be offended by some of the content. I will directly attack some of the "sciences" and current business practices in an effort to open your mind to common sense perspectives. I will explain the basics of lean and dissect management processes like Six Sigma in an understandable way. I will introduce you to an accounting process similar to lean accounting that will change the way you look and think about everything. And after much controversial bashing of the status quo, I will show you how to succeed through managed control.

This book is not intended to be a technical book on specifics or provide numerous examples of applying lean, management, or sustainable methods to prove their validity. I am not going to reinvent the wheel on topics that have been written about hundreds of times; I am going to consider their continuously similar results as fact. This book is intended to explain a process that will reach a goal, explain each step in a very basic understandable way, and provide a clear picture of what lean, sustainable, personnel management, and supply chain really are.

This book will not contain anything specific about strategic planning, market segments, demand (other than meeting it), or anything else related to selecting what product or service you should offer. There will be nothing in this book about ensuring your product is of high quality, many company's base their business model on low priced lower quality products to address specific market segments.

While I am not a psychiatrist, I will heavily discuss these types of topics because they are an integral component of business used and often misused by other non-psychiatrists within our companies every day. Many of these non-psychiatrists shape hiring practices, company culture foundations, and management directives on behavioral topics they do not entirely understand and were originally derived by marginal ambiguous research. How can people believe there is a one size fits all method to behavior and employee quality prediction? Even the attempt to create one completely baffles me.

Toyota will be mentioned in this book like numerous other books, they have done wonders with lean production and propelled their company from one of the smallest auto manufacturers to one of the largest in the world. Toyota's well-documented processes and all of those people squawking Japanese terms like parrots are not universal solutions to everything, and neither is Six Sigma. In the attempt to truly understand the history of several commonly used methods today it is not hard to find Toyota methods that were derived from Ford's methods and renamed to fit the Japanese language then modified and translated (sometimes poorly) back into English for our understanding as a Toyota method. Or we just stick with the Japanese terms. We have a terrible desire to slightly alter the existing and pretend nobody has ever seen one before.

If we step back and look at business today, we can quickly understand that profit and success rely solely on competitive advantage and innovation. Since anyone can provide what you do the day after you start doing it, what will keep you in business two days later? The simple facts are if your company is bloated with waste, has outdated products, inferior personnel, bad management, poor up and downstream communication, or negative public perception, you won't be. And I am not stating bad in all things, you can be good in all those topics, but if your competitor is comparable to you in all those things but better than you in even one, you are in trouble.

We are going to address these topics but be forewarned doing what everyone else does or creating processes that can be accomplished by primates will not be our goal. A secondary point of this book is to help students and laymen understand subjects like lean, Six Sigma, environmental sustainability, the various Toyota methods, and other subject matter that is often misunderstood or implemented incorrectly.

The real question is can you accept the way everyone does it, the way we have always done it, good enough, don't rock the boat, and culture fit are all terms leading to mediocrity and eventual failure? How can you be better than your competitors if you are always trying to achieve acceptable through conformity of the industry status quo?

This book was written to help give a competitive advantage to all forms of industry, or maximum reduction in cost for government and non-profit entities. It should be understood the amount of gain received appears to be less impactful for service and custom type industries than production industries. Though any gain over your competition is still a competitive advantage. The most significant gain from implementing the contents of this book seem to come from companies in distress, situations where the complete commitment to something different is the only chance for survival.

We must keep in mind that the processes applied and outcomes received contain as many variables as life itself. This is not the simplicity of accounting where implementing the proper steps always leads to the expected outcome of a balance in numbers (not that accounting is not complex). To completely understand what is going on here you must come to terms with the fact this is not about fixing one specific problem or another, it is about control. This is about realizing every action and expenditure impacts the entire company in some way, and all employees have a strategic thinking value.

Since the end result of a service or production oriented company can be considered their final product, we are going to consider the terms service, product, and production inclusive of all types of industries from this point on so I will not have to type "product or service" for every example or process discussed. I am not going to dance around and imply the information in this book is some new revelation handed down from God that nobody has ever thought of before. Well, at least not all of it. I almost hate to say that this book was created to ensure a lean and sustainable company because those terms have been plagued with misinterpretations and erroneous negative connotations. Regardless, lean and sustainability are the heart of the book.

While I consider the field of Organizational Behavior (OB) to be a vital field, it is very young, poorly funded, and has virtually no requirements regarding multiple replications of studies to prove a hypothesis. The typical scientific guidelines to go from hypothesis to theory do not exist in behavioral sciences; they will go from hypothesis to theory in as little as one or two studies. People behave differently from one to the next and that premise alone will never permit there to be laws within the field of behavioral sciences. Everything produced by the OB field is a best guess or assumption from hindsight that results in probable or possible future behavior, NOT universal fact.

Management books (including parts of this one), research studies, popular industry beliefs, software justification, and many other resources the business world uses to form policy and procedures are generally the result of single, similar but not exact, or unreplicable studies. For some reason, we readily accept these results and opinions as fact instead of probability.

One of my favorite OB published articles is "Pseudotheory proliferation is damaging the organizational sciences" by JEFFREY M. CUCINA AND MICHAEL A. MCDANIEL published in the Journal of Organizational Behavior online July 13, 2016. The general topic of this report is the current trend of scientific publications to discourage the repeat testing of current theories and encourage theoretical contributions. They point out that today's organizational sciences "theories" are in reality hypothesis or at most pseudotheory with rare exception. In other words, the OB scientific journals are pushing for excitement and entertainment value to encourage funding over repeated testing to prove validity through repeated identical outcomes. And the Journals additionally endorse ambiguous details of expected results that make these pseudotheories hard if not impossible to disprove.

I do obtain a tremendous amount of insight from OB articles. One of my favorites is the unintended consequences from a bus company that decided to pay drivers based on the number of passengers they picked up. The results were bus drivers who only worked during the peak times like to and from work hours, skipped stops that did not have enough people (even if you wanted to get off the bus), and would at times crash buses into each other to be first to a profitable stop.

Organizational Behavior can give us great hindsight into unintended consequences and probability of behavior to help guide our decisions. My point is that just because someone calls it a theory and claims that it is the best option, they can't prove or at times even replicate that outcome. This should not be how the business world accepts fact. We should take everything from popular authors to the most prominent institutions with a grain of salt instead of face value at this time.

The contents within these pages make up what I call the Cipher Method. The Cipher method is a management process that has some specific universal applications for every business type, applications that need to be selected based on specific need, and applications you will need to customize to suit your management style. A combination of control, imagination, common sense, and experimentation with the truth of math and consensus of policy to balance risk. The Cipher Method is about achieving a majority market share and maximum long-term profit.

Chapter 2

Surreal

Every business exists to make profit, but simply making a profit is a short-term goal. The primary goal of a company should be a profitable majority market share for each product offered. Having the majority market share gives you advantage and control over the competition through buying power and pricing. Excluding short term advantages of invention and popularity, to achieve majority market share a company must have the competitive advantage.

Without going into great detail explaining competitive advantage, I will simply point out that machinery, processes, methods, software, and other publicly available tools or information applied in an identical way as your competition will not result in any possible advantage. The key to majority market share relies solely on your employee's ability to innovate and utilize those assets more efficiently than your competition.

There is little need to cite research proving today's business environment is mostly reliant on innovation and competitive advantage. Even advantages created by innovation are short-lived if you do not have the competitive advantage because your competition will be replicating or improving on your process and creating substitutes or alternates about five seconds after your

9

product is released. So, what is the only thing companies have to ensure they create the most advanced innovations with the leanest production possible to secure their competitive advantage? Employees.

This leads me to conclude that employees are a company's most valuable asset. I do not believe I am going out on some controversial limb with that statement and need to provide volumes of research data. If we take this line of thought as fact, then why do so many companies begin this search for top talent by arbitrarily limiting their talent pool in the name of cost reduction and personality? Between our interpretation of studies, our desire to create the ideal utopia, and people's desire to sell books and processes, we have completely limited our resources. Somehow, we have cultivated the idea of having the ideal personality to fit within a perceived cultural setting is more valuable than talent and the most economical process to find these people always achieves the greatest results.

Let us examine the process most companies use today to find the best employees available to ensure their market share over the competition.

First, a low-level employee, or worse, a low-level employee from a hiring agency, submits a general advertisement that rarely has input from the positions immediate supervisor and is often cut and pasted from other previous advertisements posted. Qualifications within this advertisement often include irrelevant and limiting subjects like education minimums (requiring a bachelor's degree over experience), industry-specific software experience that could be trained in a few days, unassociated technical or licensing preference (looking for a state certified engineer when neither engineering or certification is a job function), and so on.

Then computer programs are used to further reduce the applicant pool based on arbitrary criteria and keyword searches. You just eliminated and never received an award-winning industry-specific expert resume because they did not pass the automated requirements for whatever reason. I have seen this happen more than once. Are you really going to tell me that you use a third-party service that uses standardized computer word search software to filter your applicants? There are currently degrees and certifications in my specific field that did not exist when I started in the industry, how would this scenario fit in your keyword search?

The next step is either a computer or low-level employee reducing the applicant pool further based on previous wages (I could write a page about the fault in this hypothesis), overqualification, education, and experience that the software or recruiter may not fully or even partially understand. The hiring industry boasts about their five to seven second average time to review a resume (It takes me three times that to read my own resume, much less fully comprehend the contents of someone else's.) if they have even bothered to look at it at this point. Maybe they have simply focused on the cover letter that is supposed to contain specific writing and behavioral characteristics that have nothing to do with positional talent. Google has hundreds of sites dedicated on how to write an acceptable cover letter so you can meet these arbitrary requirements.

If you are lucky and pass this gauntlet of reduction based on reducing processing labor, a phone or video interview is set up. Nine times out of ten this first stage interview is conducted by a first level employee asking canned questions (found on google) to assess your personality, communication skills, coping skills, and other behavioral traits. Being technically qualified to do the actual job is usually the least discussed topic, and the interviewer may not even understand what the job entails outside of what is on their job description.

If you passed what I disparagingly call the cheerleader test, your resume might actually be reviewed by someone that has some experience in hiring (for five to seven seconds) and either a second phone/video or a face to face interview will be scheduled. This is generally the first time a company will have relevant technical questions about the position and hopefully someone that comprehends the answers. There is usually still a large amount of personality bias at this point of the process, unfortunately.

Tell me a time when you ?? and if by some chance have never had an issue like the one they are speaking of, you better make one up. Where do you see yourself in five years? Being your supervisor is not the correct answer. In fact, most make up fictional stories or practice the expected appropriate response. The functional purpose of these questions is completely lost when they are expected and answers are not spontaneous or truthful. Basing our decisions on lies and practiced answers to meet expectations doesn't seem like a great way to select the best talent to me.

I am not going to continue with the hiring process beyond this point. The goal was not to explain the entire process; it was to give a visual of how your company is determining what makes the final cut in representing the most talented individuals available in their field. Do you firmly believe that the above process will ensure you have selected the best option available to you? If not, that missed opportunity may be realized by your competitor, but you probably have the best Google using conformist available.

Happy and other terms like "good cultural fit" are in the eye of the beholder at that point in time and may have nothing to do with what is best for the long-term company survival. We went from looking for people who thought outside the box to people who only fit in our box. What is your desired result? A bunch of happily fake people doing ok or the best talent available, even if that includes some current socially undesirable personal aspects? While this in no way includes disruptive or abusive people or customer-facing employees requiring certain positive or market focused qualities. We should use judgment based on preconceived productivity results, not preconceived cultural results.

There is a tremendous difference between selecting the best cultural fit from the most qualified and selecting the most qualified from the best cultural fit.

I am in no way stating that personality and other behaviors should not be a determining factor in hiring. I am suggesting that the weight of those attributes is incorrect and the time to determine and weigh their importance is exceedingly premature, with exception to some customer or investor facing positions. I additionally want to point out that easily trainable or obtainable factors like industry-specific software or certain certifications that can be accomplished in a couple of months even weeks should not be a reason to limit your options. They can be noted as preferred and weighed comparatively later in the process but should not be an automatic disqualifier early on.

Since I have mentioned the cover letter, I should take some time to explain why I find the reliance on the cover letter an error in early candidate disqualification. Besides finding the numerous Google sites mentioned to show a person exactly how to tailor one to meet your superficial needs, they serve no function. What position does the applicant want? The one they applied for or any you may offer. Why do they want to work for you? Because you will give them a paycheck and most likely benefits. What do they know about the company? Who cares as long as they know the job. How much smoke can you blow up an interviewer's ass without sounding too self-centered? Ok, maybe a cover letter has this one function if you are looking for the smoke blowers or fake it till you make it candidates.

The information normally found on a cover letter should be used for follow-up questions. Ask for the information you want to know during the phone interview or send a follow-up questionnaire. Do not waste everyone's time at the beginning of the process looking for just one more excuse to not look at the resume.

References, is this the 1970's? If a person does not want to let their current employer know they are looking for other opportunities, what would they do? Or in some cases industry references would mean suppliers or competitors. This is why references usually equate to friends and relatives pretending to be something they are not. Vandelay Industries anyone? Yes, I just injected a Seinfeld reference into a business book. If people have legitimate notable references, then a letter will be attached to the application. Asking for references in the beginning is just a silly waste of time and requiring them for application is an absurd talent limiter. Exceptional talent may choose to move on to another advertisement before finding and filling out this irrelevant information. Even if they intend to return to it later, there is no guarantee they will.

Experience, do you believe a recent college graduate with no experience or even a college graduate with moderate experience trumps someone without a degree and extensive experience? Amazon considers two years of Amazon employment equal to a college degree in several of their job advertisements. I am a firm believer in a college degree or equal experience requirements, but I have also seen these criteria listed in job postings where the software auto disqualifies for no degree anyway.

To try and add some perspective to my point, I would like you to realize the following founders, co-founders, and CEO's resume would never be bee seen by your hiring staff if they were automatically disqualified for not having a college degree:

Evan Williams (Twitter), Richard Branson (Virgin), Russel Simmons (Def Jam), Michael Dell (Dell Computers), Ralph Lauren, John Mackey (Whole Foods), Amadeo Peter Giannini (Bank of America), Andrew Carnegie, Annie Beiler (Anne's Pretzels), Barry Diller (Fox Broadcasting), Benjamin Franklin, Charles Culpeper (Coca-Cola), Dave Thomas (Wendy's), David Geffen (Geffen Records and DreamWorks), David Green (Hobby Lobby), David Neeleman (Jet Blue airlines), Dustin Moskovitz (Facebook), Henry Ford (Ford

Motor Company), Hyman Golden (Snapple), Ingvar Kamprad (Ikea), Kemmons Wilson (Holliday Inn), Rachael Ray, Richard Schulze (Best Buy), Steve Wozniak (Apple), and so many more.

While I am on the topic of education, what does your company consider an acceptable college degree or certification in the first place? Does your company consider online schools with the same weight as brick and mortar schools? What about private versus state or accreditation, will any accreditation do? Does anyone even check for or understand the differences in these topics?

I discount any degree from a solely online school back to the level of a high school or associates degree and do not count any solely online obtained certificates period. The reasoning is that without live onsite proctored tests you can't prove who did the work or if the requirements were even industry acceptable.

In 2009 Chester Ludlow obtained his MBA online, an extraordinary accomplishment considering he is a dog. In late 2013 Peter Smith obtained his MBA online, he is additionally a canine. Many will argue that these degrees are from unscrupulous diploma mills, but my question is how does an interviewer discern the difference in quality between online and onsite degrees?

People make a living going to online college for other people regardless if the school says it is grounds for expulsion, even exams proctored by video can be controlled by a third party. Additionally, there are no federal regulations concerning accreditation services or many certifications. You could form a company tomorrow, make a website, and start selling schools accreditation

16

status and Six Sigma Master Black Belt certificates. All things are definitely not equal in this arena.

I understand that it is easy to reduce cost by reducing the labor to process applications and that some positions can generate thousands of applicants. I am just pointing out that you will get out of the process what you put into it. Are you carefully determining your auto-rejection criteria through communication and a complete understanding? Or, are you creating blanket requirements based on assumption without any real understanding of the position? Maybe you are letting a third-party software determine what is best for you? Maybe the real reason you use personality testing is to justify an easy way to reduce your workload? You must decide what your return on investment really is, is your goal mediocrity with a pleasant attitude or the competitive advantage?

My preferred method of recruiting experienced employees involves the following steps:

1. Immediate supervisor or department head collaborates with human resources to determine position title and expectations, mandatory requirements, preferred requirements, and any indirect or secondary experience considerations. (I laugh at the ones that say master's degree preferred. No kidding, your exceptional talent felt a need to include they would prefer a master's over a bachelor's.)

2. Immediate supervisor or department head provides human resources with a detailed job description and relevant interview questions.

3. The human resources or talent acquisition person researches the local industry compensation average for the position. If the available funding

for the position resides at the lower end of the average, management should be informed of potential quality issues.

4. Pay range should be set and included in the advertisement. If existing employee's pay ranges are below the advertised rate, you have internal issues to address. This step is an acceptable way to reduce your employment pool by eliminating applicants expecting a higher pay rate. I do not care if someone made less all their life, I care that they are qualified. Basing any type of expected savings on NOT advertising the pay range is a time and resource wasting game for both parties.

5. Prepare the advertisement in basic simple terms that address real expectations and qualifications.

6. Be specific in stating the required qualifications and experience.

7. Ensure auto disqualification settings only include the required qualifications and experience criteria. Your application process should either confirm or deny your mandatory requirements including alternates.

8. Do not require submission of a cover letter or supporting documentation at this time.

9. Advertise the position internally and externally for 7 – 14 days. If the applicant pool is low or unacceptable, evaluate why and correct in reposting.

10. Contact the applicants that met the mandatory requirements to complete more detailed online questionnaires or testing (including behavior if you must) and provide supporting documentation with a cover letter.

11. Collaborate with the supervisor of the position to reduce the applicant pool further.

12. Select 10 or less to phone interview (face to face internal applicants). This should be to evaluate BASIC comprehension and communication skills, plus specific positional knowledge based off of step 2 provided questions.

13. Collaborate with positions supervisor to reduce applicant pool to an acceptable face to face interview quantity.

14. Conduct face to face interviews with at least one human resources and one position supervisor representative.

15. Any further steps typically required.

There are no reasons why application can't be a two or three step process. A second step online process will allow you to create and evaluate what is essentially their first project for you. Think for yourself and create an efficient process that guarantees you are selecting the best available without limiting the applicant pool through superficial requirements. Do you absolutely need candidates to have a college education or do you simply prefer it? Do you need certain certifications, or do you simply prefer them? My primary concern is direct and indirect experience over anything else unless certifications are required to perform the job. Education and any other skills are a secondary measurement with personal opinion of behavior a third level concern.

You can't pretend you will always hire the most qualified forward-thinking people through the most economical process available. Computer software does not have AI sufficient to judge people, recruiting companies are marginally better than software but are still removed from the company's best interest, and inexperienced recruiters are simply inexperienced. Later I will discuss the 5 why's; this is an excellent method for determining required and preferred qualifications.

Investors, boards, and senior level managers often say that they want self-sufficient leaders who think outside the box with an entrepreneurial drive to move the company forward. Investors and the board of directors may whole heartedly mean this, but what they get are managers looking to meet profit goals without getting fired. In fact, most hiring managers will not even call an applicant with business ownership experience, a business owner's next in command has about a 1000% better chance of receiving a phone interview request than they do. Everyone says that they want these specific qualities in employees then view it as a negative in the hiring process. Hiring managers dismiss or avoid applicants with these credentials under the reasoning of overqualified or assumptions of attitude. Why do companies consider overqualified a negative? Fear of replacement or the belief that these leaders will become bored, argumentative, disenchanted with the current bureaucracy, or rock the boat in general. Isn't that what we want, to find fault and improve our processes?

If top-quality employees are bored, then there is a problem and they will offer solutions. If there is reasoned bureaucracy they will accept it, if there is excessive bureaucracy they will offer solutions. If they are rocking the boat, then maybe alternative views with experienced debate are what you need to stop being average. Any leader that does not welcome competition, debate on alternative views, or dismisses others ideas in general, is not worth having.

When we look at quality employees being a positive towards increased income, we all know that it is not as simple as just hiring the best available at any cost. Fully staffing a McDonalds with MBA graduates is not going to increase their profit above the expense for doing so. And there are no mathematical formulas to guarantee the cost of a superior employee is going to result in less expense or greater revenue. But to determine the expected quality and cost of an employee that will provide the maximum return on investment requires us to have a quality employee to make these decisions in the first place. It is a very circular conundrum, finding exceptional talent requires exceptional talent and effort.

We currently accept psychology-based research to guide us because it is politically correct, not scientifically sound. Then we inject financial games based on budget over talent. While I am not saying neither has significance, I am saying the current reliance on flawed policy to limit our available resources is counterproductive to achieving greatness.

I believe that hiring primarily based on personal or supposed psychology-based testing to ensure a culture fit, limits talent for no proven reason and is a guaranteed way to remain average. I thought Amazon was going to be my main example of how to hire correctly based on their acceptance of two years employment equal to college degree requirements for certain positions along with their actual process testing. But never fear, they had to throw in personality testing too. When posed with the question "Are you rude to other people?" the entire premise of the test just went out the window. Tell the truth and not be hired because of it? Guess at what they want to hear? The statement of we gain a lot of information based on how long it takes someone to answer a question is a big pile of bull, another attempt to justify garbage hypothesis with more garbage hypothesis.

Psychology based reasoning may be presented as fact, but we need to understand it is often presented with little research and ambiguous parameters to serve a selfish purpose. Most psychological hypotheses are formatted in a way to prevent being disproved. Prove your god exists vs. prove my god doesn't exist. You can spend years arguing what all of the variables are and why each point has reason or is invalid. Please view psychology-based information as a probability or possibility, NOT FACT. Your business culture did not improve because you hired cheerleaders based on behavior testing; it improved because certain behaviors became unacceptable and management was resolute in supporting this cultural shift.

Hiring needs to be based on qualified human judgment of ability from the maximum applicant pool available. Pay needs to be based on the industry average with flexibility to retain existing quality employees. Talent and common sense, a fight to overcome the easy way.

Tell me about a time when you convinced your CEO hiring is as important to having a competitive advantage as lean production.......

Chapter 3

Finders Keepers

It is not difficult to understand that if we do things the exact same or worse than our competition we are failing to secure the market share. If we are not gaining, we are either losing market share or stagnant and vulnerable. It is not hard to state that employee quality has a direct impact on all the factors mentioned. If your employees are equal to or worse than your competitor's quality of employees, how could you ever expect to be better?

You could randomly throw a rock inside a bookstore or library (if those still exist) at the business section and hit a book about the "levels" or "stages" of leadership. These authors usually divide leadership into four or five categories with descriptive words like executive, unitive, pinnacle, and so on describing the upper level of quality leaders. These descriptions are fine, they are useful tools, but in my opinion, the top level is something that comes from natural ability and cannot be successfully taught to anyone, and not what I am about to discuss.

There are three categories of business leaders – Type I creators, Type II improvers, and Type III managers.

Type I – These are individuals who create successful companies from the ground up without safety nets. In other words, they are all in financially and failure usually means bankruptcy or worse. This risk allows for a deep and personal understanding of risk and opportunity. The education of all business segments through trial by fire, where errors directly result in personal financial loss, where the true realization of the need for replacement training and employee dedication exists, where success is only realized through wealth, and stress is above compare.

Type II – These individuals are similar to creators but have personal or family wealth as a safety net. To meet the requirements of an improver, you merely have to significantly increase the existing family wealth. Knowing that you will not be living in your car if this idea fails and the typically dominate interaction with people backed by wealth creates a different outcome and understanding than a Type I creator. Bill Gates, Donald Trump, and Elon Musk are all famous improvers.

Type III – This is where most of today's typical corporate world falls. These are people whose only experience is from managing companies that they did not create or have a majority stake hold in. Creators and Improvers can be managers, but managers must quit being managers for a significant time period to find out if they are creators or improvers. It is the experience and goals that make managers different from creators and improvers; managers are more about using other people's money to reach a predefined financial goal or superior's recognition. They have no or limited financial stake in the game outside of employment, and success is narrowly defined. Their understanding of the big picture and risk is limited comparatively.

Type I leaders are focused on long term results, while short term goals are often necessary to initially stabilize finances. Creating a legacy is generally their primary objective.

Type II leaders are primarily focused on the long-term goal of lasting personal success recognition. A need for accomplishment to prove their status is earned.

Who is to say which is better, a creator or an improver? They are very different in many ways. The mindset of having to make a company work or you will be ruined financially is obviously different than starting or buying companies with risk that is comparable to most of us buying a car. Type II leaders rarely re-enter the corporate world below the C-Suite level because they can afford not to.

Type III leaders are focused on the short-term goals of annual investor expectations and continued employment. While the goal of personal success recognition exists, the scope of recognition is confined to the primary short-term goals. Type III managers are the area where the "levels" of leadership apply because creators and improvers are all proven leaders of superior accomplishment while managers are leaders of predetermined goal accomplishment. Pushing people to be exceptional Type III leaders requires training and education to grasp the concept of good or great leadership.

Why is discussing the types of leaders important? To gain a perspective on true experience and vision over perceived compliance as success. My point is that you can have a "pinnacle" level leader that only understands the goal of meeting investor expectations and following industry norms, who successfully leads the entire company into obscurity. There is far more to lasting success than making people want to follow you off the cliff.

Let us look at one of the most famous Type III leaders of recent times, Jack Welch the former CEO of GE Corporation. An engineer brought up through the ranks to become CEO, resulting in change and tremendous growth. While most business students and executives know who Jack Welch is, it is not a Bill Gates or Elon Musk fame.

If you take a close look at what made Jack so successful, you will see many of those aspects in this book, like quality employees. You could say Jack was an example of the highest leadership level, but I believe a better example would be a Type III leader with Type II qualities. He took some risks to achieve goals, but in the end, it was not his money and failure would have simply resulted in unemployment for a financially stable individual. If it was merely about his methods being followed like a one size fits all rulebook implemented by handpicked replacements, GE would not be plunging towards the penny stock designation today. Jack was successful because of his natural ability and vision to push boundaries, implement new ideas, and use innovative strategy.

Next, I would like to take a look at Sears, Amazon, and Walmart. Amazon is not some revolutionary idea created out of thin air that is making department stores like Sears obsolete. Amazon is a modern-day version of Sears in the

1890s and Walmart is somewhat a progressive version of Sears from the 1980s. You see, Sears was on track to be both the Walmart and Amazon of today, but type III managers completely failed to hold on to the majority market share and were decimated by a couple of creators, Sam Walton and Jeff Bezos. Though Mr. Bezos may be considered by some an improver instead of a creator due to his family's ability to loan him $250,000 in 1995, I consider him a creator.

This is what the Cipher Method hopes to prevent, the death of companies by attrition created by investors demands of stable mediocrity from complicit managers. There is a solution, but that solution requires defining acceptable risk and ensuring true leadership vision.

While Type III leaders struggle with thoughts of being replaced or surpassed by their underlings, Type I and II leaders realize the potential for increased output with less personal effort from quality replacement training. Type III leaders can be incentivized to change their replacement perception through evaluations and incentives based on direct report competency. If failing to ensure every effort is taken to cultivate your replacement is treated as a negative, the perception will change.

Type I leaders have a great sense of ownership and must succeed to survive, Type II leaders have the finances and control to push through risk-averse boundaries, and the few famous Type III leaders successfully implemented progressive change originally developed by Type I and II leaders. The answer to a successful business lies in finding leaders who are more than a typical Type III leader with some charisma for senior positions. Leaders that understand including and cultivating employee success equates to company success instead of personal competition. Only then can you truly believe people are being hired, promoted, and trained based on their potential, instead of avoided because of potential threat.

I have addressed the current standard hiring practice of relying on the least experienced personnel to determine your employment pool. Or worse, hiring a "recruiting agency" that is even further removed from your actual needs. All typical recruiting companies do is advertise for the position and send you what they get after repackaging the resume to make it more attractive to you. I found one job being advertised by three separate recruiting agencies and none of them could tell me details about the actual company or position, not because it was confidential, they simply had no more insight than what was available on the company website. Their only goal is to sell you whatever they can get you to buy, not what is best for your uniquely specific needs.

Once we evolve past all the hiring games used as an excuse to not thoroughly evaluate candidates true ability like secretive pay ranges, behavioral based interviews (including the STAR method), seven-second resume reviews, cover letters, blanket positional requirements without supervisor input, and stereotyping based on race, appearance, previous salary, and so on, we can move on to retaining these qualified people. Believe it or not, there is a multitude of companies that have no idea how to do this, or simply do not care. And on the other hand, some companies look at the cost of replacing an employee more burdensome than keeping poor employees.

Sometimes Toyota will require external management new hires to work in the departments they will oversee for months. This is to allow the future manager to understand the company and processes before they take the position they were originally hired for. Toyota believes in promoting from within first, but when that option is not viable they spend months of resources to try and inject the experience. Toyota is additionally known for requiring cross-department training for management consideration. There are no better qualifications than knowing and understanding the company process and culture first hand.

Most companies sit and shake their head in agreement with the benefit of internal promotions and cross training, right before they figure in the cost. Knowing that an exceptional employee or at least one who has been showing up on time with limited sick days wanting to cross train is often rejected for the unknown in the name of cost savings. If this person leaves to work in another department, they will have to be replaced and both positions trained. A new hire could come trained and possibly hired at a lower rate than the existing employee. What is your choice? Agreement with having known employees trained in all aspects of your company is best, or the more economical unknown dedication and segregated duties?

We need to face the realization that the days of employers stating requirements and expectations for a pay scale and then detaching themselves from the relationship outside of recorded facts and figures are over. These historical ideals of tyrannical rule, military obedience and hierarchy, or governmental equivalent bureaucracy, generally result in a revolving door of employees in lower power distance areas like the United States. The only direction for success is to create an atmosphere where everyone from top to bottom is working together to achieve success, and those that are not providing a benefit are replaced sooner rather than later.

Several books and studies show that compensation is not the primary reason people leave their jobs, bad management is. This does not mean compensation is not a factor; it means that when weighing the balance between compensation and dissatisfaction, dissatisfaction overwhelmed compensation. This does not equate to paying people more so they will tolerate greater dissatisfaction before looking elsewhere for employment. Compensation versus dissatisfaction is a very disproportionate scale where compensation escalates exponentially compared to dissatisfaction. This leaves the sensible action of managing dissatisfaction to control cost and retain valuable employees. Unfortunately, many misinterpret satisfaction to mean happy.

Yes, I am well aware of some popular studies by renowned universities stated the obvious fact that a positive work environment is shown to be more productive. And as usual, people translated positive to mean happy and started to treat this as some law of nature. This misguided trend began to push company culture to be reflective of imagined personal utopia. Not that I disagree with having a positive company culture, I insist upon it, but not to the point talent is sacrificed for exuberant cheerleaders.

Before I expand on the specifics of employee retention, I would like for you to think about the following employee perspectives. Most employees enter your workforce with a positive attitude hoping for a satisfactory work environment that will last for a long time; it is up to you to develop the relationship. Your employees have personal lives and responsibilities, and many employees will experience some of the worst days of their lives while in your employ. Will you support or abandon them? There is a point where you have to cut the cord so to speak for the benefit of the company, but how you determine these values and limits will resonate through the company impacting dedication. Additionally, business has no room for racism, gender bias, or affirmative action. These topics are counterproductive to ensuring the highest quality employees.

This can be a difficult area to manage without acceptable communication avenues in place. Is Molly just a negative bitch, or has she simply adopted that personality to prevent others from constantly taking advantage of her willingness to help? It should be easy to tell when someone is being deceitful or negatively affecting others with the proper management process in place; we are merely skipping the ridiculous idea that being happily fake towards other employees somehow benefits the company.

For thousands of years we have been compensating people for their service through chickens, money, stock options, medical insurance, trade, or other forms of bartering. The amount you should compensate someone for their services in a particular position is not an industry secret; the internet allows employees to find the industry average with the click of a button today. For this reason and the ones previously mentioned, I am not going to further address the idea of fair compensation to retain quality employees. If you can't figure out how to click the same button your employees and potential hires do, then your problems run deeper than we can fix here.

I am going to address employer-employee expectations. This is not about the initial employment agreement stating pay, benefits, and position expectations that usually include the blanket statement of "additional duties as assigned." This is about behaviors, goals, boundaries, and general expectations both parties agree to. Long gone are the days of companies dictating what acceptable behavior is, generally in the form of hollow "treat people with respect" statements that equate to accept the supervisor's bad behavior (if it is legal) and stop complaining. Suck it up.

Type 1 & II leaders understand that competent, well trained, and free-thinking employees allow them to be in more places at once and they understand that these dedicated employees are required for growth. And most of all they understand quality employees free up time to focus on other issues or simply enjoy the fruits of their efforts. It is a simple formula; if I can train and retain someone to do my job, I can either focus on something else or simply do less in general. Type III managers struggle with the thought of being usurped and must push past those feelings, if you truly understand business then you understand good managers are judged by the success of their direct reports. I am sure you will find that great leaders are quite lazy on some level and micromanagers spend more time managing than accomplishing.

The business world has so many types of statements even I get confused which means what or is specifically important to my perception of whatever. Then you add in the eloquent all-encompassing positive words that make the company sound like a selfless saint that results in a big pile of bull nobody believes anyway. You can call this organizational core values, mission, culture, or anything else you like; I am going to call what I am discussing the Company Conduct Agreement. Not to be confused with a company's code of conduct, typical codes of conduct are an employer mandate that serve a function. This is not a code of conduct replacement.

Company Conduct Agreement – An agreement of shared values, goals, behaviors, and expectations of the employer-employee relationship.

This agreement should be created by employees and not senior management. Senior management should have no to minimal input in the companies conduct agreement creation outside of the President or CEO final approval as a company directive. If created by the employees, they will have ownership in the success of the company and self-enforce the agreement. The failure of employees to adhere to the agreement leaves little room for argument when replacement is required. This is the first step in employee inclusion to the management process that will promote success in many other areas like sustainability and lean processes.

These are the guidelines for a Company Conduct Agreement:

1. Delegate any employee below senior management to form a team that will guide the process. This team should include employees from all levels of employment and a diverse representation of departments. This team should form subgroups if needed to gather information and input from the employees as a whole in a meaningful way. How to form these teams is up to you, volunteers, elections, even lottery.

2. Instruct these teams to create self-explanatory single sentence value statements with a detailed explanation for each to the primary group. Single-word values like "Respect" are too ambiguous, "Treat all with respect" is simple and understandable without room for interpretation. Sentences that need a paragraph to explain them are discouraged. Values like "Freedom and responsibility within the culture of individual discipline" may equate to some wonderful values that could propel the company to greatness, but who really understands what it means without explanation.

3. The primary group should evaluate the submitted information and select five to ten final statements to make up the Company Conduct Agreement. One value should support the FIT culture mentioned later.

4. The primary group should submit to the employees for comments.

5. The primary group submits the final draft to the president or CEO for implementation.

Now as the president or CEO who has just been handed this list of conduct values your employees have decided are the best conduct guidelines to ensure the success of your business, what do you do? Picking it apart, dismissing it, or failing to enforce it sends a clear message that you do not think very highly of your employee's ability. Sure, you may have some questions or want to discuss the reasoning behind it but be very careful about imposing your will.

After the Company Conduct Agreement (CCA) is approved by the president or CEO, the companywide implementation should begin. Posters of the agreement and other artifacts should be posted in multiple visible locations, opportunities to recite the agreement should be encouraged (before or after meetings, events, etc.), and enforcement of agreement violations should be swift and meaningful without retribution for doing so. In other words, if the lowest level employee mentions that the president is violating CCA #3 by berating him, even if during said beratement, no negative consequences should arise from it. It is up to management to lead by example.

This brings us to the topic of termination. It is no secret that terminating an employee results in costly replacement and lost training investment. The only key here is consistency in enforcing the policy. Besides keeping Sally for missing over the acceptable amount of work time and firing Fred for the exact same thing will get you sued, it sends mixed messages and is a sign of poor management. Some companies create a policy that makes it nearly impossible to terminate a sub-par employee, and others create a reasonable policy like three strikes and you're out but do not enforce it properly. Far too often what is supposed to be a two write up and coaching before a final warning offense, often skips the first two warnings and goes straight to a final warning or termination when you piss off the wrong person.

I live by the one warning and coaching followed by termination for repeating the same offense, and three supervisor complaints or negative reviews additionally result in termination. I believe that the cost of replacement is far less than keeping a sub-par employee one day longer than needed. I am not going to be specific in my general policy regarding termination because every business is different. My stringent rules would most likely result in constant understaffing in the fast food industry. My advice here is that whatever

35

your policy, do not keep poor employees for the sake of replacement expense and be consistent.

Since I have mentioned coaching, it may be time to open that bag of worms. I am sure the original intent of the term coaching was to encourage managers to fix minor issues with direct reports job performance. Today it is more about blaming a bad hire on a manager's inability to coach them into a competent employee. If anyone is stating that an employee continues to perform below expectations because they need more coaching or better coaching than a proven supervisor just gave them, your problem lies someplace else like policy, hiring practices, or wage rate. If a call center supervisor spends more time coaching previously trained employees to do a simple repetitive job, the problem is not the supervisor and repeated coaching is just wasting time and money.

Every person is different; we all have different expectations, behaviors, knowledge, intelligence, natural ability, tolerance, and temperament. What line of thought leads us to believe that limited engagement and assumption of ability or intelligence based on position ensures the company's maximum return from its human resources? It completely befuddles me to try and understand why countless hours of coaching are spent to try and make poor employees reasonably competent, but we only talk to competent employees once or twice a year during mandatory reviews the manager visibly considers an irritation.

What exactly is it we expect from our employees? Do the employees know what we expect from them? What do the employees expect from us for doing what is expected from them? What can we do to help employees meet expectations? Since all of the above is in the form of questions, I hope the answer is fairly obvious, communication.

What can we do to help employees meet expectations? Let us assume ignoring, being dismissive, and having a superior attitude is not the answer. I am not going to cover topics like compensation, work and life balance, unusual workplace amenities like video games or skateboard ramps, and so on. There are other books about these topics, but I must remind you of the previous discussion concerning their validity. My reasoning for excluding these topics is that compensation is self-explanatory and not always an employee's primary concern, my wife would be ecstatic over the occasional mylar balloon, ink pen, or a free T-shirt. Work and life balance are in my opinion, not a valid topic because some people are happy with putting in a challenging eight hours and leaving the cell phone on the desk until the next day, while others dream about the middle of the night call to help. The only challenge is determining who prefers what and not chastising the person who leaves work at work unless it is part of their expected duties. And some artistic type jobs like advertising benefit from employees having a mid-day work distraction of games or skating to clear their head. These are topics best left to your experience.

Our concern is the connection between management and employees. When competitive advantage can come down to fractions of a penny per piece, we must realize all employees are a major component in maintaining or increasing that fraction. Sally is having an off day or is in general disgruntled with her employment, can reduce profit. And ignoring Bob's idea because he is a line worker and you do not have the time, could be lost revenue potential. If we are going to look at fractional cost savings in material acquisition, energy cost, production time, transportation cost, and so on, why would we ignore the human aspect?

You do not need to ensure that Sally is happy 24/7 or that you assign a group project for every one of Bob's ideas. You need to manage your people as intellectual assets cultivated to achieve their maximum output. You need to make downsizing a term only used when dropping a product line or a downturn in the economy reduces demand. If you are reducing employees to save money and make the financial return numbers look better, you have a serious management problem.

As I mentioned, it is not your job to ensure Sally is happy 24/7, but it is your job to understand Sally and see if there are easily correctable or preventable factors associated with her job satisfaction. And Bob may come at you with a new idea every day, but if one out of a hundred of those ideas saves the company ¼ of a cent for every 100,000 parts produced it is your job to identify it. How you accomplish this without wasting 10 minutes a day listening to him is an example of your management prowess.

It is not hard to prove most people just want to be heard, included, and taken seriously. I believe a majority of people just want to voice their issues and being able to do so eliminates a majority of their discontent. But in today's world, we have companies that only do yearly employee review sessions where the manager doing the review often openly displays his dread of the task. Review policy that grades performance on a number scale where managers are prohibited from assigning the highest score. And pay raise policies that advocate losing employees regardless of their history and ability if it exceeds the base annual percentage increase allotment.

We create environments where employees are subjugated instead of included and tie the hands of managers doing reviews. It is no wonder many managers dread reviews when essentially all they are doing is evaluating with the objective of finding some fault to encourage "improvement" and checking a box to approve the yearly cost of living pay raise.

The following procedures should be implemented to ensure employee communication and inclusion.

- Have a minimum of two direct supervisor face to face reviews annually.
- Have an additional minimum of two employee satisfaction electronic surveys annually, alternating the face to face reviews.
- Have one anonymous reverse review annually through HR. Reverse reviews from the HR department help prevent the issues of favoritism and cliques or what is commonly called "The good old boys club."
- Have a system in place for employees to submit cost reduction or improvement ideas that are actually reviewed by people knowledgeable in the subject matter and have the power to implement. Incentives are a plus.
- Provide a confidential venue for employees to report inappropriate behavior or find direction in personal issue resources.
- Make Human Resources (HR) personnel readily accessible and knowledgeable in all employee-related topics.

There is no proof that always finding an area for improvement or never giving someone top evaluation scores improves output. Employer reviews should only serve the purpose of rating the employee's output compared to the supervisor's expectations. If a supervisor does not give the highest rating then they should have an honest and productive reason to give the employee, "I am not allowed to give a 5" is never an acceptable answer. Either employees earned their maximum annual rate increase, or they didn't, making it a cost-saving game is counterproductive to employee satisfaction.

The proponents of always finding areas of improvement and never give the top scores are guided by erroneous silo vision. They do not study the impact of these negative assessments on employee's morale, only the benefits to their hypothesis. Telling a stellar employee they do not get to have a top score for their efforts because you can't give one, equates to the management being unappreciative and instills a lack of motivation in the employee to continue excelling because it will never be recognized. Always finding room for improvement can equally result in a lack of appreciation and overall discouragement. Several people have described their reviews as a slap in the face and lose faith in being recognized by a fair and attentive employer deserving of their dedication.

Knowing that reviewers can't give top scores and must find areas of improvement no matter the performance negates the flimsy reasoning for doing so in the first place. Needing to improve in an area is just something they had to say, and if I waste time working on that, they will just come up with something else next time. So why bother? Why bother with going the extra mile because they will always score me the same and give me the same pay increase as "only does what she has to" Nelly over there.

How about this crazy thought, evaluate people based on their performance and suggest areas they really need to improve if any? Build trust and improve your employees based on accurate, relevant reviews. Games, games, games everywhere.

Walk and observe – This is the same as Toyota's Gemba Walk. Even if you personally did the work previously, things change. Familiarize yourself with what is being done today in both production methods and culture. The less you leave your office, the less you know.

It is hard to argue that reporting on or resolving problems requires a full understanding of the problem. Making assumptions just makes you an uniformed ass. Not only should you familiarize yourself with day to day activities, you should observe until you fully understand the reasoning for your processes. Your superior trusts that you have a personal understanding of the situation, not a second or third-hand perspective reliant on hearsay.

We also use these walks to better understand the current state of our employee culture, and promote the concepts of accessibility and inclusion. There are no downsides to spending time in the trenches, other than time, and I would argue anything else you need to do doesn't have a better ROI. Toyota managers will walk around the plant and stand quietly in designated spots for long periods of time observing employees and their processes without ever interacting with employees. This is believed to give managers firsthand knowledge of the manufacturing process and evaluate changes or problems.

Training – We need to understand that training is a management responsibility. If an employee acts in any way other than what we want, we have failed. If we react negatively to an employee doing as they were trained, we have failed on many levels. If we make concessions to trained processes, "It is not important to do it that way," then we have failed before we started.

To clarify, training someone to know when they should stop a production line is not free will, it is an operational procedure. If you provide clear expectations and thoroughly train personnel in the process steps you require to achieve those expectations, all outcomes should be as expected. Free will has nothing to do with independent responsibility.

Inactivity – There is another historical line of thought we need to change, inactivity is always bad. If an employee is not doing anything other than sitting and waiting for their next task, it is not always a bad thing. The problem with "keeping people busy" is that they are often not where they are supposed to be when they are supposed to be there. Someone sitting idle while waiting for a process to end could be waste, but their idleness is not the problem to correct, the reason for the long cycle is.

It is fine to assign additional tasks that do not detract from the main objective, like having a receptionist prepare bulk mailings at her desk. But having the receptionist help set up a meeting room takes them away from the entrance and the phones. You have just made the receptionist ineffective at their primary duty.

Look at it like firemen, fire person? Fire people? Anyway, we all pay them to sleep, eat, play games, and so on for most of their day. But they also maintain their equipment, stock supplies, provide public safety services, and complete other relevant tasks. Most of all, they are available to respond to emergencies when needed. Imagine how upset we would be if they were doing road repairs to fill time and had to go back to the fire station for their equipment before responding to an emergency.

Your press operator is there to operate (and hopefully maintain) the press; it doesn't matter if that function has a large amount of inactivity as long as they are there when needed. Sure, there are things that they can do, but those things better not waste one second of production time because they are not there when needed. If additional duties to eliminate idle time cause one defective part to flow through the line because they were not there, or equipment failure that could have been prevented or limited with them there, you are creating waste.

Inactivity is not always bad; this line of thought has been proven to eliminate waste numerous times.

I brought up the concept of the three types of managers to point out the companies everyone works for today are in existence because of creators or improvers. Creators and improvers have a mindset and culmination of experiences that could never be taught to others. The fame of people like Bill Gates, Elon Musk, or the late (2018) Ingvar Kamprad compared to the relative anonymity of all Type III leaders with very few exceptions, indicates that there are fundamental differences in types of leaders. One of the rare Type III exceptions, Jack Welch of GE, helps us realize handpicked and mentored replacements ensured to follow a predefined set of steps, or general attitude does not equate to continued success.

You need better than policy driven automatons to be a superior company. You must do better than just say we want entrepreneurs, self-starters, innovative thinkers, and dedication. You need to cultivate and support those qualities through effective communication, inclusion, and example. Make success based on more than financial goals, bureaucratic policy, and militaristic hierarchy. Use your human assets to their maximum potential. Use the long-term goals of type I & II leaders to create success instead of simply meet expectations.

We additionally need to look at the internal position of change management. Many of us think of someone in charge of a major change within the company when we think of the title change manager. This is not always the case; most of the work done by change managers revolves around the normal day to day business operations. Change managers are more like internal PR managers, or IR (internal relations) managers? Besides major changes like switching to lean principles, any change within the company has a better success rate if a change manager becomes involved. Studies show that the success rate increases the earlier a change manager becomes involved.

How many times have you dedicated resources to evaluate new programs or processes that fail for no reason when implemented? Well, there may be a reason, maybe it failed because nobody was onboard with the new program and decided themselves that the old way was just fine. Change managers help prevent this.

Chapter 4

Lean, What Does it Mean

There is a term being used today that I have already used in this book and will continue to use throughout, lean. Unfortunately, the term lean is often misunderstood and misapplied. For our purposes, I am going to give you two definitions to clear up what lean means to us.

Lean – Operating and producing without waste or reduction in quality.

Waste – Cost or resources that can be avoided.

Here are some examples of what lean is NOT:

- Reducing labor through downsizing to save money. Lean methods generally try to avoid reducing the labor pool.
- Automation. Lean methods sometimes prove manual labor is better than automation.
- Partial implementation by selecting individual tools or areas of improvement. Lean is a continuous effort, more like a lifestyle that should be ingrained into your culture. Just implementing a couple of tools like 5s or Kanban does not make you a lean company.
- Mass production. Lean may be used in mass production, but they are different things.

- The avoidance of union labor. If the flexibility of duties and pay schedules (mostly bonus incentives) is possible, unionism has less impact on the process.
- An advertising point to increase sales. Lean is not a term that should instill a desire to choose your product over another. Your superior price point, quality, and on time delivery resulting from lean are what you should advertise. Using the word lean to advertise products means you do not understand the term.

Companies often misuse the term lean to describe reducing the budget by any means. For an office to be lean it must mean every aspect of the office functions are being met at maximum quality (including work environment) without waste. Reducing cost by reducing your workforce resulting in increasing workloads to a point quality, output, and morale suffers is not lean.

Like the terms product or service that I combined to the word product for simplicity reasons, we need to do the same with the use of production examples or topics within this book. Lean was originally linked to the production process because so many of the existing terms and methods were written with production in mind. We have come to realize that most if not all these methods work equally well for just about any type of business application, including human production in an office environment. If I am using an assembly line example, you may need to use your imagination to see how this same process may benefit your office, hospital, store, maintenance crew, and so on. This would be a very long book if I gave examples for every sector that I could imagine.

Quality is subjective, but we are going to give it a finite definition for our purposes. **Quality is the customer's perception of satisfaction, or a measurable fact that the next product or service delivered is equal to or better than the previous product or service of the same name delivered.** In other words, anything you do to reduce cost must not reduce the quality of your product. I doubt anyone will be upset if lean measures improve the quality of your product.

Your product can't change to a lower quality due to lean implementation. My printer Model X purchased today is expected to have the same print quality, ink cartridge, speed, life expectancy, and options as the Model X I previously purchased. The latter model X can have fewer or more moving parts, do more than the previous one purchased, or any similar change that does not reduce my expectations in comparison to the first one purchased under the same model number.

Another example would be reducing personnel cannot change or lower the expected quality. If employees receive a certain level of response from human resources one day, then lowering the number of employees in human resources the next day can't reduce the level or quality of response the employee's received the previous day. And the same goes for customer expectations.

Unfortunately, this is where lean gets confused with cost-saving changes. Changing something that results in lower quality is change not lean. Our fast food industry has changed its product over the years to reduce cost through mass production, longer shelf life, and simple assembly. If you believe that these hamburgers, tacos, etc. are of the same quality today as they were 30 years ago, then it was lean improvement. If not (I am a definitely NOT) then it was change.

Recently my favorite lunch spot, a locally famous pizza chain, started to have abrupt changes and lost my two to three times a week lunch business. They had a great lunch price for several combinations of their products; I had three favorites I would rotate through, pizza, sandwich, and chef salad. Then out of the blue, my lunch special totaled $1.40 more than usual. I pointed to the sign and said, "I think you made a mistake." The young man said "Oh, I need to take that down. Corporate is making some changes." He still gave me the price on the sign that was so old you could see where the prices had been covered over by yellowed masking tape and handwritten with marker several times. But the reason I stopped going was not the sudden 15% price increase.

I stopped going a week later because they had removed the black olives and onions from the chef salad and changed the meat on my favorite sandwich to a thinner cut and more processed version. All I could do was imagine some idiot at an office thinking that they were implementing lean when they were just trying to save money by screwing up the product. I hope they choke on that extra nickel they saved on my salads and sandwiches because I will never buy another one. What set them apart from my multitude of choices is now gone.

In very basic terms, a purely lean system repeatedly produces defect-free products, with equal quality, in quantity equal to demand, at the lowest possible production cost. We accomplish this by eliminating waste in our company. One way of looking at this is waste equals expense, and we need to strive for zero expense without reducing quality. An impossible goal that should produce impossible results.

Waste is anything we do or spend money on that is unnecessary for creating and delivering our product. Examples would include:

- Defective parts
- Lawsuits
- Walking further than needed
- Waiting
- Having to find things
- Communication barriers
- Storage
- Utility waste
- Material waste
- Excessive management

There is an infinitely long list of things that could be considered waste, but the bulk of it comes in the form of wasting time, wasting utilities, wasting materials, underutilizing employees, and storage cost.

A process for improvements that I live by is to look at what you are doing and prove that you are doing it wrong. If you say that every step of every process you have is wrong and someone must prove that it is wrong, what are the possible results?

- It was wrong, but proving it was wrong has given you the answer of how to do it right.

- It was right.

And when you are finished proving every step was either right or wrong and made needed process changes along the way, you need to start over because those changes may have changed the answer for previously tested process steps. If you didn't make any changes then you are probably doing it wrong, so you better start over anyway. There should never be a day when attempting to reduce your cost of doing business by improving your process stops at good enough. If it does, that is the day your competition starts to catch up or surpass you. Constantly working towards this unachievable goal like an addict looking for their next fix will result in improvements in all areas of the company.

Do the wheels need to be placed on the automobile first? We have always done it that way so the vehicle can roll down the assembly line. Today the answer is no; the wheels are installed much later in the assembly process. Can you imagine the first guy who had to convince corporate that installing the wheels later was more efficient?

This is not a process similar to purchasing new equipment and expecting immediate results; it will take months to see results and years to master. Failures and setbacks are to be expected, but initial large out of pocket monetary investments are not. The question is not when we should start? The question is, have your competitors already started?

Since corporations are basically viewed as a separate legal entity in the United States, the human body serves as a good analogy point. A major concern for people (business) today is their weight (waste). To keep our weight low (lean) we understand that we must monitor our consumption (creating or accepting waste) and exercise (continuous improvement). We additionally understand throwing money at this issue is not a permanent solution. Weight loss happens slowly and being lean is more of a lifestyle choice than anything else. Yes, I understand that for some it is a physical or mental issue that prevents weight loss (I have never been accused of being thin), but if we equate this to our analogy, poor operating management seems to fit.

While I am blatantly using analogies, I need to address some common analogies misused in this field. There has been a trend to use the analogies toolbox and tools to represent methods or processes used to become lean, out of context they can be misleading. There is a long list of "tools" that we will talk about and I will continue to use the term tools, though a more exacting analogy for many of them would be tool accessories. The issue arises when procedural systems like Six Sigma call themselves a "toolbox" in an attempt to promote themselves as a universal answer to every business need. The truth is Six Sigma is not a "toolbox," it is a "tool" that has specific uses and alternatives, alternatives you may prefer or work better for your situation.

All of those tools you hear about like Kanban, Poka Yoke, Andon, and many more, are all parts of various puzzles and are not intended to be a complete solution. When I say parts of various puzzles, I mean that every company is different, and you need to form a picture that suits your needs. You will need several "tools" from the toolbox, but not all tools will be in your best interest. For instance, not every product or service type should be produced by a pull system, so trying to implement Kanban is not the right thing for everyone.

You will need to look at all of the available tools and select the ones that work best for your particular environment. You additionally need to understand picking tools one at a time and executing them to an expert level before you focus on the next is not the proper way to become lean. If we expand upon our previous human analogy, tools are equivalent to our dietary and nutrition plans or exercise equipment. You would not watch your calorie consumption one week and then just focus on vitamin intake the next week, you would do both at the same time. And you would not take an entire bottle of vitamins at once to cover the monthly intake, you would take a small amount daily.

There are some universal tools that everyone should start to implement immediately. In the beginning, Google will have adequate information to start using these tools, and specialty consultants (mentioned later) are not necessary at this point.

5S – Sort, Set in Order, Shine, Standardize, Sustain (A little clunky due to Japanese conversion)

The basis of the 5S method is to create an obsessively clean and orderly environment to eliminate various wastes and ensure problems stand out. Have you ever watched tv shows like "The Prophet," "Bar Rescue," or the various save the restaurant shows? They are implementing lean tools, and the first is usually 5S.

The first step Sort is to mark every single thing you have with a priority based on immediate need, near future need, and keeping it around because I may or may not need it someday, or it is worth something because I paid money for it but rarely if ever use it.

The keeping it around because I may or may not need it someday, or it is worth something because I paid money for it, needs to be sold or thrown away. WHY? Because it is costing you more money than it is worth through storage cost, employee time having to look or work around it, and the time value of money aspect. Your idea of having $100,000 worth of stuff crammed in every nook and cranny is costing you more to keep than if you threw it away or sold it for next to nothing. I am not going to waste two pages convincing you this is true, just do it.

Next is Set in Order, placing everything you kept so it is accessible and easily found.

Now we need to Standardize everything by creating procedural steps that everyone follows to ensure everything stays in its place, like the outline of tools on the pegboards we are most familiar with. These outlines not only tell us where something goes, they quickly tell us when something is gone. A place for everything and everything in its place.

Shine is self-explanatory, clean like everyone has a compulsive disorder. It may feel like you are wasting time by ensuring everything is clean all of the time, but it has been proven that you are saving time in the long run.

And Sustain simply means you ensure your standardizing procedures are being followed. That the entire five-step process is a natural process ingrained into daily behavior. Some people include a 6th S for Safety; many argue that if the previous five steps are properly followed safety is a natural result.

To make a long story short, everyone should know where everything is and when it is missing, nothing should be "in the way", performing a needed function should take the least amount of effort possible, and you should be able to eat off the floor in every area from the office to the manufacturing shop.

I had one professor tell a story about a previous supervisor who considered having enough email in your inbox so it initiated the scroll bar as unacceptable clutter. Not only did he believe this, but he would also periodically check and reprimand for the offense.

5 why's? – Root cause analysis tool.

The five why's are a take on our natural trait from childhood to ask why when learning about the function of our surroundings and life in general. Yes, this tool encourages us to act like we are five years old and ask the question of why up to five times.

This tool will allow us to fully understand the root cause of problems instead of taking knee-jerk measures that may not solve the issue.

Example: A certain station is underproducing,

1. Why is the station underproducing? Because the machine has a high defect rate.
2. Why does the machine have a high defect rate? Because the operators are inexperienced.

3. Why are the operators inexperienced? Because operators quit or ask for transfers from this station.

4. Why do operators want to leave this station? Because it is hot and uncomfortable.

5. Why is it hot and uncomfortable compared to the other stations? Because the machine creates heat and there is poor air flow in this area.

As you can see, the first why could prompt you to replace the machine, the second why may have prompted you to pay for additional training, but the last why revealed the root problem of airflow. Not all problems require you to ask why five times and running around asking why a bunch of times may feel silly, but it is worth it in the long run. Embrace your inner five-year-old.

Changeover Management (Not the same as change management) – When changing from one type of production to another, or as basic as preparing a hospital room for a new patient.

This is where you reduce downtime for production changes like die or equipment swaps. If it takes you a day or an hour to make these changeovers, you need to reduce them to zero. Ten minutes is the typical industry goal. Yes, this is one of those impossible goals that have been proven to have impossible results.

In settings like hospitals, it would be reducing the time to prepare rooms for the next patient. This is a great example of how a process created for changing over manufacturing product lines and molds can be used by numerous other industries. If you are thinking that you can understand where saving a few minutes setting up a hospital room would save on labor when the volume of rooms is considered, you are only partially correct. The real savings is in the reduction of wait time for patients to be placed in the room. You are eliminating wasted time in your process and increasing the flow of patients, or at the very least increasing your maximum production output capabilities.

Changeover times are greatly reduced by preplanning, standardization, and performing tasks that can be done beforehand. Standardizing the materials needed like tables, screws, tools, etc. will save time. Preparing tools, equipment, and materials needed beforehand will prevent looking for stuff. Doing tasks that can be done before and after the machinery is running will save time. Planning routine preventative maintenance like replacing common failure points (hoses) during this scheduled downtime will prevent future unexpected downtime. Even creating your own tools or equipment to facilitate faster changeovers is a common practice.

Value Stream Mapping, Spaghetti Charts, and Root Cause Analysis tools – Understanding your current processes and defects.

Value stream mapping is simply creating an organizational chart that maps the journey and time raw materials take to become a finished product. You can map any process like this; it does not have to be a product. You can value stream map your customer complaint or purchasing approval processes, basically anything.

Spaghetti charts are the detailed mapping and timing of tasks or actions. For instance, when a company changes production from one product to another, people usually physically perform a set of tasks. These tasks may include switching machinery or dies, rearranging tables, adding equipment, and so on. A spaghetti chart will have a continuous line that follows each person involved throughout the change and includes the time for each task along with travel time between tasks. The lines often look like a mess of spaghetti when complete, imagine what a map of your day would look like if there were a big pencil on your back drawing a line on the ground as you moved.

I mentioned the 5 why's earlier as a root cause analysis tool, but the 5 why's are more of a behavioral process than what I am talking about here. This is about using fishbone diagrams, scatter plots, and so on when brainstorming. Visual aids to help understand the root cause of issues.

Below are some additional tool and industry terms including short generalized descriptions. Please remember, you use these tools to help become lean, you are not lean just because you use these tools.

6 Big Losses – Six main areas of loss in a manufacturing system. Breakdowns, Setups & Adjustment, Idling, speed loss, defects, startup.

7 Wastes – The seven typical places waste can be found, Overproduction, Inventory, Transportation, Motion, Waiting, Defects, Overprocessing.

80/20 Rule – (Pareto Principle) – A hypothesis that states 80% of the effects come from 20% of the causes and is strangely true more often than not when applied to most anything, including nature. This is not a Law, it is not always true, but it is often a useful tool to find root causes.

Andon – (Japanese paper lantern) – The use of visual signals on the production floor (or other places) to relay information that can be quickly interpreted at a distance.

Backorder – A backorder is when you are delivering product past the date promised. Several custom products are built to order and the expected start to finish time is called lead time, something is not on backorder until it is past the stated lead time or demand is greater than supply.

Bottleneck – When a single stage of a process takes longer to complete than any other stage. When corrected it is possible for a bottleneck to move to another stage. Example: Put three clamps with different amounts of pressure on each clamp along a water hose. The end result will be less water coming out of the end. Remove the tightest clamp (bottleneck), and more water will flow out the end of the hose, but the hose is still restricted by the second tightest clamp that is now your new bottleneck. And so on until all clamps are removed eliminating your bottlenecks to achieve maximum "continuous flow."

Brainstorming – Creating a solution or developing an idea through group discussion.

Cause and Effect Diagram – (Root Cause Analysis) – Flowchart of a process to find faults.

Cellular – Arranging production in groups to increase overall output by reducing cycle time and creating a continuous flow.

Continuous Flow – Free of bottlenecks or other issues that cause delays in production.

Demand Management – A process to help predict demand.

Demand Smoothing – Ensuring production operates at a steady pace by utilizing pricing, promotion, and other means to diminish seasonal or cyclical effects.

Energy Management – The act of monitoring and controlling utility usage to ensure minimal waste.

Fishbone Diagram – A visual root cause analysis tool.

Green – Typically used when describing the use of material that has been recycled, repurposed, or otherwise environmentally friendly.

Heijunka – A tool to regulate continuous flow to meet demand.

Hoshin Kanri – A tool for meeting strategic planning goals

Jidoka – (Autonomation) – Creating automatic processes to detect defects and either signal an alarm, stop production, or a combination of both.

Just In Time (JIT) – Production is limited to actual or projected orders. Nothing is produced for surplus inventory purposes. The pure form of a Pull system.

Kanban – Regulation of the material flow in a pull production system using signals to indicate when supply should be replenished.

KPI – Key Performance Indicators – To track and encourage progress towards goals.

LEED - Leadership in Energy and Environmental Design, is the most widely used green building rating system in the world.

OEE – Overall Equipment Effectiveness – A tool for measuring productivity loss.

One Piece Flow – Creating a complete product through a production line opposed to creating pieces of the product for later assembly.

Poka Yoke - (Japanese for mistake-proof) – The act of creating a system that prevents mistakes. This could be as complex as lasers to ensure the assembler reached into every required part bin before the production line will move, to ensuring all required fields are filled in on a form before submission.

Pull – Production quantity based on actual or estimated orders.

Push – Production quantity based on keeping inventory.

Note: Some industries are a combination of Push and Pull. Auto manufacturers are one example: cars are both made to order as a primary objective with inventory production as a filler to keep a continuous production flow.

QFD - Quality Function Deployment – Determines customers primary wants and uses a matrix to signify the best plan of action based on the input.

Queueing Theory – The mathematical study of predicting and reducing queues/wait time.

RFID – A radio frequency identification system to accurately monitor inventory location and quantity.

Scorecard – Used to track and evaluate overall vendor quality.

SMART Goals – A goal-setting tool.

SMED – Single Minute Change of Dies – Changeover Management tool that applies to more than changing dies. This tool is often used for understanding the benefits of reducing the time to complete any type of changeover.

Takt Time – The pace of production in relation to demand.

TPM – Total Productive Maintenance – Training machine operators to help maintain their equipment.

TQM – Total Quality Management – A system to ensure quality products and customer satisfaction.

Variance – A fluctuation in the production process that prevents continuous flow and exact replication. Examples would be dies that wear out causing increased thickness or human inconsistencies causing time variations.

A real-life example of variances and the effect on time would be traffic. If nobody else were driving on the road, it would take you far less time to get to work, but others are driving on the road so the time to drive to work varies a little (sometimes a lot) every time you drive to work. Not to mention stoplight patterns. Now imagine you have a service company where the product requires you to drive all day, how could those variances change your output?

Have you ever noticed how people leaving after a light turns green do not all start moving at the same time? Your variance in time to get through a stop light depends on the people in front of you, and sometimes it even depends on if the cross flow of traffic stopped at their light or tried to hurry through.

Visual Management – Using visual aids to convey messages or direction. (See Andon)

Value Stream Mapping – Flowchart of activities

There are many other terms and adjusted terms to fit some particular company's need or attempts to promote "new" ideas. I wanted to point out the primary terms related to the topics within the book and some of the most significant industry terms needed for an emerging lean company. There is no need to spend a tremendous amount of time and energy on Andon, Heijunka, Jidoka, Kanban, OEE, and others until you have evaluated and adjusted your production flow at least once. And I purposefully left out some management tools like Six Sigma because they will be addressed within specific chapters for proper context.

Ever wonder why automobile models only had significant changes every decade or so and now it seems like major changes take place about every other year? Because the old "over the wall" design process would take about six years to design and implement major model changes. The "over the wall" design process consisted of someone making a design and "throwing it over the wall" so to speak, to the engineers, and then the engineers would find problems and throw it back "over the wall" to the designer. Then the designer would make changes and throw it back over to the engineers, after this happened a few times the engineers would then throw it over to the suppliers who most likely throw it back due to issues. This cycle would repeat over and over to eventually include assembly, cost concerns, customer appeal, and so on. Lean and communication concepts realized that by putting everyone together at the beginning (designers, engineers, suppliers, assemblers, customers), issues could be realized sooner, and the time saved reduced the ability to make major model changes by years.

Another often overlooked advantage of being lean is flexibility. A truly lean company should be able to reduce production instantly to meet any downturns in the market without having excessive funds tied up in a large inventory of materials or finished goods. Or completely relocate with minimal expense due to the various speed bumps life throws at us like labor issues, government regulation, shipping concerns, political climate, resource availability, and so on.

Chapter 5

Supply Chain is Everything

What is Supply Chain? Most people think of their supply chain personnel as the people who order stuff. While this is a function of the supply chain, that line of thought is like saying electricity is only used to run your lights. Hopefully, you take advantage of electricity to run other things like heating and cooling, refrigeration, television, and so on.

I believe that Operations Chain would be a better designation, but I will work with what we already have. Your supply chain people are responsible for your chain of material from mining the ore to the last minute of the final product warranty, even if your company is not the original or final producer. They are additionally responsible for the internal and external gathering of information along with monitoring procedural steps. Supply chain is equally responsible for the amount you pay for staples, where the staples are, that you have enough staples, and the efficient flow of production in your facility. In any given day, the person in charge of your supply chain operations could worry about paper prices, why there are so many procedural steps for an accountant to order pens and the variances between workgroup A and B on the assembly line.

Today your supply chain functions fall under a very wide umbrella because the relatively simple task of ordering product now has an expectation of reducing the cost and amount of product needed. Besides ordering your packaging paper, the supply chain is tasked with ensuring you use as little paper as possible and that the process to request paper itself is not wasting labor. It will even go as far as ensuring that the paper supplier is not wasting material or labor to ensure your cost is the lowest possible, and that they can deliver quickly so you can reduce the amount of paper in inventory.

Your supply chain does not stop at your door, it continues upstream to ensure your suppliers, and at times their suppliers, are operating to your standards and need. Upstream communication with suppliers is vital to material cost savings and limiting the amount of material on hand needed for short-term production. The thought bulk pricing saves money has not only been proven incorrect, it has been proven this line of thought costs tremendous amounts of money. You should stop buying in bulk for the sake of cost savings immediately.

We need to ensure our suppliers are operating as lean as possible to reduce our cost and ensure we receive product when we need it. We additionally need to ensure that suppliers are in line with our CSR (corporate social responsibility) goals. Buying product from an environmentally harmful company can directly reflect onto your image. I am not going to go into the history of proving that working closely with our suppliers reduces our cost. Instead, I am going to give you a couple of examples of the extent companies go to trying to limit storage, shipping, and production cost.

A professor told me there is a building located near a large auto manufacturing plant housing three separate companies working together. These three companies all specialize in a stage of windshield production. What they realized is if they combined under one roof near the plant, money could be saved by making the windshield production a continuous flow. Things like heating the material to make the glass then letting it cool for shipping just to be reheated again at the next facility for cutting and shaping turned into a single process. Now the glass can be made and shaped without (or limited) the waste of reheating or shipping. And being located near the plant they can produce to demand with very short distance shipping. Everyone increased profit through reduced cost and environmental impact in numerous ways by working together.

While attending a supply chain presentation, a local company discussed how they calculate the statistical math to ensure a local soft drink manufacturer has their cans delivered on time. You may be thinking, why would you need to hire someone to do math just to ensure your cans are delivered on time? Because the manufacturer has their supply-demand figured out down to the minute. The required number of cans has to be delivered in a projected 15-minute window or the entire plant shuts down. I found this to be fascinating. A major soft drink company has figured out that the risk of shutting down the plant is less costly than keeping excess inventory. Their production demand is so precise they can project need within a fifteen-minute window. And their suppliers are more than happy to comply.

Another upstream advantage that seems odd at first glance is reducing the number of suppliers you use. We find that forecasting and optimizing inventory along with creating personal relationships with suppliers willing to meet your demands and cater to unforeseen circumstances is more cost-effective than creating competition between multiple suppliers of varying use. A great relationship with a lower number of suppliers that can meet your needs will benefit you in many ways even if it is not always the lowest price. While price is no longer the singular primary concern, it is still a concern. The local utility company, Ameren, reduced suppliers from 35,000 to 8,500 and rave about the benefits of the end results.

Supply Chain is responsible for the downstream customers to ensure you are receiving the information you need for optimal production and customer issues are addressed. Downstream customers can be significantly important to help regulate your demand, reduce cost, and reduce finished goods inventory. This efficient production from understanding actual demand can increase the maximum output of your process allowing you to sell more. The more you know about your customers and their customers actual demands, the better off you are in projecting your actual demand needs for all customers. Downstream customers will additionally benefit from lower stock warehousing cost and reduced or eliminated stockout issues.

This communication will additionally help prevent the bullwhip effect. The bullwhip effect is where a customer orders a large amount of safety stock on a regular basis making the supplier think that their demand is greater than it really is. This causes the supplier to order more inventory from the factory which now has a false perception of demand and orders extra raw materials to satisfy the suppliers demand, and so on. Then the bubble bursts and the end user or retailer realizes that they have too much of the product because of safety stock and stops ordering it. This unpredicted drop in orders leaves the upstream suppliers with a large amount of unwanted stock. It is more complicated than that, but you should get the idea.

The waste created from safety stock is a subject to address immediately. People become so concerned with running out of a product for use or sale they will order extra and literally hide it. You could have thousands of dollars in materials, product, or supplies hidden behind things or above your ceiling tiles. Yes, I said above ceiling tiles. Audits often find that what was assumed to be stolen is really being hid within the facility for possible future need. The main problem is this product is not monitored and ordering an extra 10 to squirrel away for an emergency can accumulate to 100 without realization. Then you need to consider some items can expire or be forgotten about altogether. Responsive upstream or internal suppliers help eliminate this problem when people know needed items can be obtained quickly.

There are numerous reasons to communicate in both directions of your supply chain. Wasted material can be reduced by asking your customers if product sizes or styles can be altered to gain the greatest use of material sizes or machinery restrictions. If those cereal boxes could be made with different dimensions while keeping their volume, we would have less waste and could share the savings with you? It happens more than you would think.

The reverse can also be true. One story talks about how a computer manufacturer was able to save money and improve their product by just asking their supplier about a better part. The part was actually less expensive than the one they were currently using because it was being mass produced for European customers due to environmental regulation changes. A simple phone call allowed for a reduction in cost, faster delivery times, improved environmental impact, and an improved product feature.

Hopefully, you understand my point; control over your cost does not end at your door. Trust is also a major factor in accomplishing waste reduction in suppliers; you will need to know things about each other that might be considered sensitive information. A hurdle you may need to overcome by taking the first step.

You would assume that any good-sized company would have a supply chain department or at least a person responsible for the companies supply chain as mentioned above, but you know what they say about assumptions. I visited a very large "healthcare opportunity" company (They provide and distribute medicine along with managing programs) who showed me their super-fast lean prescription filling process. Machines did most of the labeling, sorting, and bottling work, but humans still prepared and inspected the medicine before it is dumped into one of the hundreds of bins in the machinery.

Afterword I asked several questions about waste I could still see in their process when it became clear that there was no supply chain department. The task of reducing waste was the responsibility of each department and often took a back seat to their primary duties. Sure, they had made great strides in their efforts to get the product out faster, but good enough became the norm. Continuous improvement was replaced with leaving it until senior management pushes it.

Making money hand over fist does not equate to making the maximum amount possible.

Returning to my human analogy of a company, management is the brain, production the heart, sales the lungs, and supply chain is the circulatory system. We need all of these things to survive, and even one in poor condition impacts the others.

A major bump in the road today is the fact supply chain, the field that covers most of what this book talks about, is a very new field of study in universities. When I started my degree, the emphasis area was in Operations and Logistics Management and the university renamed it my junior year to Supply Chain Management and Analytics. It has been over a century since Henry Ford started figuring out the benefits of lean production (Mass production is different and developed later in Ford's history) and decades after Toyota published their lean methods before we started to recognize supply chain as a focused field of study.

If supply chain is a relatively new field, who is running the supply chain divisions of today? Primarily people with economics or finance degrees. I take my hat off to these pioneers educated by fire, learning a new concept through self-education and various consultants that started their own consulting companies after working for Toyota or other industry giants. But the supply chain is about far more than economics and finance, the time of figuring it out is over.

It may seem like everything is now being arbitrarily thrown under the supply chain umbrella, but if you take the time to think about it, all these things either directly or indirectly impact the cost, quality, and quantity of output. Even returns or lawsuits reflect on the cost of production. From the supply chain perspective reducing defects has very little to do with the promotional aspects of a product, it is about eliminating the expense of returns or reworking material. The public perception of a defect-free product is just a side effect that benefits sales and increases demand.

A term that I need to address because I often use it is "efficient production," a goal of the supply chain division that has been misinterpreted for so many years it is one of the supply chains biggest perception challenges to overcome. Since the advent of mass production, the term efficient production became synonymous with the idea of producing as much as you can as fast as you can because the cost per piece declines as volume increases. In fact, this line of thought has become so ingrained, companies' base expectations and bonuses strictly on volume of output. In recent decades we have discovered that this line of thought is the opposite of efficient production. This line of thought increases defects in output (because bonused and scaled cost are based on quantity and not quality), greatly increases material handling and storage cost, and can reduce product value due to surplus. When I say efficient, I am really saying lean or without waste.

As I have mentioned previously lean and mass production are not the same thing. Mass production is churning out as much as humanly possible, and lean is producing without waste. You can have lean mass production, but lean generally means you are only producing at a rate to cover your immediate or projected need to reduce raw material on hand, finished product storage space, and financial investment. Only meeting actual demand additionally allows you to reduce possible price fluctuations due to overstock and free up financial assets sunk into product that will most likely not increase at a rate equal to the time value of money if ever sold in the first place.

At the time of this book, everyone is enthralled with Japanese terms because of Toyota's success in manipulating much of what was originally Ford's processes and procedures. Ford most likely obtained his original ideas from the works of Frank and Lillian Gilbreth who expanded on Fredrick Taylors work based on human movement to standardize production. You can even go as far back as Eli Whitney who first attempted to manufacture products (guns) with interchangeable parts. If we wanted to, we could go back to 1801 to credit Eli with planting the seed that would become the concepts of lean and supply chain as we know it today, his only problem was technology did not allow for his interchangeable parts to be manufactured well enough to be truly interchangeable.

Lean and supply chain theory faces some of the same issues as behavioral theory previously mentioned. Toyota is currently the popular focal point for much of our education because their processes to achieve that success is well documented. We find that many do not disclose specific details about achieved success in their processes due to the fear of competitor replication. Obviously, failures do not ask people to study their mistakes or run out to publish books about it.

The supply chain field does have one thing that the behavioral sciences do not, math. This is why I fell in love with this field; it is like experimenting or guessing based on experience or imagination that will always have a math formula to support or reject the probable outcome. Unintended results can smack us in the face or turn the search for a penny into finding dollars. Supply chain is a field that lies somewhere between the educational guessing of psychology and the pure mathematical outcomes of physics.

A couple of decades ago a very large computer printer manufacturer automated their plant with the intent to increase their manufacturing speed. They immediately realized that the robots were unable to assemble the products as fast as the human labor due to the need to adjust the speed down to a point the robots would not damage the parts. So, they started to redesign the printers for faster robot assembly. To make a long story short, after several redesigns the manufacturer had greatly reduced the number of parts within the printer (while keeping the same quality), and the robots were able to meet the target speed for assembly. But this is not where our example of supply chains ability to overcome a challenge ends. Somebody said let us see how long it takes humans to assemble the newly designed printer? The human assembly time was significantly lower than the fully automated time. In the end, a human assembly line still manufactured the printers, but the new speed of assembly due to redesign was far greater than the original projected automated assembly time goal. Unintended results can be surprisingly amazing.

Supply chain and lean have two major enemies, good enough, and approximation. Stopping at good enough ends in lower potential earnings and loss of market share, and approximation results in variables that reduce optimal output. When we speak in terms of averages we are saying that variables exist in our process and variables are waste that creates more waste. While variables are often unavoidable, we need to realize their impact on our systems.

To continue with a food example, imagine you have a hamburger production line. You say it takes on average 1 minute to prepare a cheeseburger. And for example sake, we will make each step the same with the same averages and variables.

Each of six steps to make a complete hamburger includes the hamburger patty, bun, cheese, lettuce, onion, and condiments. It takes on average 10 seconds at each station with a 4-second variable resulting in 8 to 12 seconds possible per stage.

If the actual times are as follows:

1. 8 seconds
2. 10 seconds
3. 9 seconds
4. 12 seconds
5. 11 seconds
6. 10 seconds

You think ok, it took 60 seconds on average to make the burger, what is the big deal? Now imagine that you needed to make 100 burgers and each step relies on the previous one to be completed before it can start.

- Burger 1 is fine at 60 seconds, but we start to see build ups and wait times extending through the next few burgers.

- After 48 seconds step 1 has created 6 burgers, but stage two is still working on number 5.
- After time stage 3 is doing nothing while waiting on stage 2 to finish because stage 3 is operating faster than stage 2.
- After a longer amount of time stage 4 is doing nothing because it is waiting on stage 3 even though stage three is moving faster than both 2 and 4. Because stage 3 is waiting on stage 2 stage 4 winds up waiting on stage 3. And this entire time stage 1 is piling up a mound of finished burgers in front of stage 2.

Yes, this is really an example of a bottleneck at stage two. But the point of the variables is that the above times will change at all stations from average to one extreme or another each time creating an unpredictable moving bottleneck. After enough time someone will have a pile of burgers waiting on them, and some will be doing nothing while waiting on burgers.

Now expand upon that and think of what is happening after 8 hours and what about other processes waiting on your finished product like packaging? Those burger wrappers have their own average wrapping and bagging time that is messed up before it starts because the finished burgers have gone from 60 seconds on average to who knows what. This is one reason your product x takes an hour to make, but you can't seem to get one from start to finish for a week.

This problem is greatly reduced by lowering the variable time, but the problem can still arise. When we must say average, we mean our process has variables creating waste. In a perfect process, each stage will take 10 seconds, and we will not be creating burgers at an average of 60 seconds each, we will be creating burgers every 60 seconds period.

There are all kinds of math formulas available to us that determine how we can improve our processes.

- Estimate our return on investment
- Estimate our reorder points and quantities
- Reduce queues and wait time
- Predict future needs
- Measure variables
- Calculate optimal labor start and stop times
- Placement of distribution centers

Just about anything we can think of, there is a math formula to help or justify it. Restaurants use math to determine down to the minute when and how many cash registers should be manned to serve customers faster, even what size tables will reduce wait times. Previously restaurants thought only of the number of chairs they could fit into the dining room, or a waitress could cover. Math has shown us that at times larger tables traded out for smaller tables equates to fewer overall chairs but accommodates more people during peak times by reducing wait times, thereby reducing lost income from people who do not wish to wait.

Another function of the supply chain department is data collection. You will quickly learn that Data is your most valuable tool in the fight against waste. You need to start collecting and compiling data on everything from the steps employees take to perform their duties to suggestion box inputs. You will additionally need to collect data from external sources like vendors, suppliers, and customers.

Today costs are determined down to the second, fraction of a cent, square foot, and kilowatt. We want to acquire all the data about every activity and expenditure involved with our company. Notice I did not say all relevant data, today all data is relevant. All lean production methods and tools have one thing in common, more data is better. We have begun to understand that what was previously considered inconsequential or an unavoidable cost of doing business is as important as material cost or sales volume.

The more data you have increases your insight and reduces your cost and guesswork. I have mentioned previously that all of this is really about control, and for control, we need to remember knowledge is power. We need to provide our departments with all the data we can, including what you may have previously thought to be trivial information.

Hopefully, we all understand that communicating with and polling our customers leads to creating higher demand products with reduced waste from focusing on the incorrect features. If not, there is a tool for that called Quality Function Deployment (QFD). We should also be familiar with vendor scoring through a scorecard to monitor vendor expectations. Both are very important data tools that you should familiarize yourself with and implement early on.

Other forms of data collection have been mentioned previously like value stream and spaghetti charts. The point of this chapter is to push the point that you need to perform these data collection processes on EVERYTHING, not just what you are working on at the time. And you need to keep this information forever.

Time is money, and if you will recall, our goal of zero expense would additionally require us to produce in zero amount of time, have zero backorders, and be paid instantaneously, among other things. We must find ways to meet these goals and data is the key. Shaving a second off one process step could save us an hour by the end of the process and equate to higher product output. Higher product output can additionally increase sales, eliminate backorders, or allow for the time flexibility to add additional product lines.

Even keeping track of failed ideas should save time if the issues are revisited, and keeping track of what may be considered irrelevant ideas is equally important. If someone submits an idea for toilet seat warmers, you may deem this a silly idea. But if over time seven people submit the same idea you may want to check into it. What if you found out that time was being wasted because the toilet seats in question are on an exterior wall that gets unusually cold in the winter, so employees are walking to the other side of the building to use those bathrooms. That silly idea might save you thousands of dollars in lost production.

No data is bad and more detailed data is better. We do not just want to know how much electricity your building uses; we would like to know how much every light bulb, electrical outlet, and everything in between uses individually. Get the picture?

Say someone makes a decision to change something, and it was a bad decision, what should we do? If a formal set of steps (like FIT mentioned later) were in place and documentation supports those steps, we file it under failed. We don't scream and run around with our heads cut off looking for a scapegoat. Our data will support the reasoning for the failed decision and we move on. Or we find fault in the process used to support the decision and change the process.

Acquiring live data – The unfortunate part about collecting data that relies on human observation is that people behave differently when they are being observed. One of the most hilarious things to watch is an employee trying to watch and document another employee without being detected. We need real-life behaviors to accurately find variables and other waste in the process. The difference between employee A's output and employee B's output doing the same task needs to be impossibly identical to ensure a steady flow. Why they will never be identical has to do with about a million human variables we could never hope to correct, but we need to know what ones we can correct, and observation is at times the only solution to finding these variances.

You are going to have to change your perception of the world around you. Sam having to take five extra steps to walk around surplus stock is waste, Billy having to walk around for ten minutes looking for tools is waste, Gertrude having to wait for a supervisor is waste, and so on. You do not want to pay for people to walk, find, or wait on others, and the best way to find this waste is through live observation.

Anyone should be able to access existing data stored in a database (I suppose a file cabinet is a type of database) when starting a new project to research what may have been previously done, worked, or failed concerning their current project subject. Every group project and improvement idea should begin with an internal data search.

Transportation is a topic I will not thoroughly address because it is rather complicated and frankly, something I would consider outside my expertise. While I am fully versed in transportation topics and have a small amount of direct experience in national and international transportation, I am only going to provide some general perspective on the topic. Shipping is a major function of supply chain and at times can make or break a company.

Beverage companies install multiple production facilities because the cost of shipping liquids long distances can be costlier than building plants and hiring overlapping personnel. The best chip dip ever created that smashes the local market could easily go out of business because shipping cost prevents expansion outside the local market. Transportation can be a major cost factor that kills a great idea in the blink of an eye.

Besides the normal issues of packaging, distance, delivery method, and delivery time, the pricing factor can be complicated. Shipping is generally limited to a predefined volume and weight determined by standardized shipping containers. You could ship ten tons of lead that only takes up $\frac{1}{4}$ of the space in the container, but the weight restrictions force you to pay for the entire container. The reverse is additionally true, 10 tons of feathers may have a volume that requires five containers resulting in five times the shipping cost of lead.

On an international shipping level, you need to deal with both countries' government regulations and procedures, not to mention complex payment agreements. Your product may not be allowed to be exported from your country of origin or could be acceptable for export but restricted from import at the destination country. Customs forms and procedures, tax issues, duty-free zones, exchange rates, international trade agreements, last mile responsibility and coordination, government stability, even piracy are just some of many topics to consider. This is where third-party providers come in, these companies called 3PL's or 4PL's (3rd and 4th Party Logistics) come into play to ease the complexity of both local and international shipping and related pitfalls.

Doing business in other countries can be a very complex endeavor. Amazon has difficulty selling in underdeveloped countries due to a lack of internet access and delivery methods; shipments are often sent to a local partner store (think of a general store in the wild west) where people can place orders and pick up their deliveries. Netflix can't seem to add China to its customer list because of government regulations that promote China's companies in direct competition. Some countries will not let outsider's own property; this results in local citizen partnerships or sometimes licensing agreements only. Some countries even have laws requiring the use of approved distributors that are legally protected in their favor.

Population Perspective:

Country	Population	Population Rank	Land Area KM sq	% of World Population
United States	329,000,000 +	3	9,150,000 -	4.27
Russia	144,000,000 -	9	16,376,000 +	1.87
China	1,420,000,000 +	1	9,388,000 +	18.41
India	1,368.000,000 +	2	14,686,000 -	17.74

Did you realize that India had nearly the same population as China? Russia has less than half the population of the US? That China has 4.3 times the number of people than the US with about the same size land mass? Another interesting perspective is on the size of the African continent. The US, China, India, France, Italy, Mexico, Germany, Spain, all of Eastern Europe, and about ten other countries will fit on the African continent with a little room to spare.

The above chart should allow you to better understand the reason for globalization. If your company only sells to the US, then you are ignoring slightly less than 96% of the world's population. For companies that do sell to the world market, single country manufacturing is simply unrealistic. I am fairly confident that the US population couldn't produce enough product to satisfy the demand of all US companies selling product overseas. I always try to buy American Made when economically feasible or even available, but in today's world, it is just an unrealistic goal to do much more than hope for assembled in the US.

The major qualities in a successful supply chain manager are perspective, common sense, drive, and imagination with a healthy dose of intelligence backed by data.

Chapter 6

Environmental Sustainability the Hidden Gem

Some people associate the topics within this chapter to the current concept of the triple bottom line or three P's, Planet, People, and Profit. I believe the triple bottom line thinking to be antiquated. We need to understand that planet and people are not separate goals from profit. Today it should be understood the way your company treats the Planet and People has a direct impact on Profit. Environmental sustainability for us is not about Birkenstock wearing hippies chaining themselves to tree's; it is about saving money and creating a positive public perception. We will discuss how being lean and being environmentally sustainable are not mutually exclusive and are often achieved within the same action.

While it may begin to sound like my focus is only on the money aspect of environmental sustainability, I do understand our reliance on the environment.

Historical anthropology has proven the human species has been destroying their environment ever since we started gathering in groups large enough to do so. Our forefathers did not have some natural sense of environmental harmony; they would deforest and farm around their cities until they became uninhabitable.

If we are supposedly more advanced than our predecessors and always learn from our mistakes, then can someone explain why the Dust Bowl happened in the 1930's? We farmed to the point of soil erosion where dust storms made three states nearly uninhabitable. It was not a new problem, we have been doing this to ourselves for thousands of years. The only change was our ability to do it in about a decade instead of centuries.

In the last 100 years or so we have not only globalized our communication and production, we have globalized environmental destruction. Issues like the Great Pacific Garbage Patch, deforestation, acid rain, and over fishing just to name a few. The Great Pacific Garbage Patch is a section of the Pacific Ocean that took the discoverer Charles Moore days to sail across with nothing but floating garbage as far as he could see.

So where will this end? When we have made the environment around our village uninhabitable and we have to move? Oh wait, we are not talking about a village anymore. I believe it is safe to say that if we have not figured this out in the last 6000 years or so, it is unlikely we will stop doing it without reason. Today the most influential reasons to do or not do anything are investor expectations, social pressure, and government regulation.

Large corporations like Walmart have championed environmental sustainability initiatives and research in the last couple of decades. Why? Because it makes them look good to the public? No. Because it saves them ridiculous amounts of money. The initial momentum usually came from companies trying to earn some goodwill with the public, but those before mentioned Birkenstock wearing tree hugging hippies put on their suits and proved money could be saved by being environmentally mindful. If you believe that Walmart is one of the most environmentally friendly corporations just so you feel better about them, you are sorely mistaken.

It seems natural to me that three goals can be accomplished here simultaneously, lean, corporate social responsibility, and environmental sustainability.

Corporate Social Responsibility or CSR is about showing how your company is impacting the outside world. CSR can come in many forms like financial donations, free access to services, reducing your carbon footprint, etc. Showing that something you do without profit (even if it may reduce expenses or improve public relations) makes life better for others, or at the very least shows that you are limiting the negative impacts from your existence as much as possible.

Environmental Sustainability is the idea that everything you create or consume as a business can be naturally replenished, biodegrade, or returned to the production cycle without diminishing the existing environment. Things like energy consumption from energy sources created from burning coal are bad, but energy consumption from renewable sources like solar or wind generation is good. Trash that goes to the dump is bad, and recycling is good. Creating a product where it or the process to create it generates toxic waste is bad but finding a way to make it or the process less toxic is good. While these are very basic examples, you should get the idea.

Like so many companies, Walmart was experiencing some negative public relations issues and decided to counteract them by implementing some environmental sustainability programs. They discovered implementing many of these environmental sustainability initiatives reduced operating cost at a very low rate of return on investment (ROI).

Until I read "Force of Nature: The Unlikely Story of Wal-Mart's Green Revolution" by Edward Humes, I was like everyone else thinking Green is a fad and environmental issues were bad, and someone should do something about that. Not me, but someone. After reading Force of Nature, I was talking about it to anyone who would listen and amazed that everyone wasn't doing this. I doubt that I can explain the financial benefits of environmental sustainability any better than Mr.Humes did, so this will be a short chapter.

How difficult is it to understand that upgrading some equipment may save you two to three times the cost of the equipment in utility savings over a fairly short period of time? A completely fictitious but generally accurate example would be spending $10,000 on lighting upgrades to save $2,000 annually on your electric bill for 10 to 15 years. Or how about implementing recycling measures that lower the amount of trash you pay to haul away, plus generates a check from the recyclable material?

Utility bills can be wrong. Some people even find out they are additionally paying for someone else utilities. Utility bills can point out easily correctable waste. Why is the water bill so high? Because the toilets need minor repair and it has never been prioritized since they still work.

A major issue is that some utility companies have different rates for the time of day and the amount used. Plus, they may charge based on your largest peak for the entire year. In other words, that day in August when the AC was running nonstop during the high demand part of the day and your largest presses were pumping out a large order, you peaked up into a higher electric rate tier and could be paying based on that tier for the rest of the year. Even if you never peak into that rate tier again. Companies that monitor their electrical consumption will often push the production time of some machinery to a second shift when the rate is lower and help flatten out their peaks. Some companies have found that it is less expensive to install and run off generators for short periods of time to prevent crossing the higher pay rate level.

The best answer is not always replacing all light fixtures with any led fixture because any led fixture costs less to operate than what you have now. Even the thought of putting motion sensors everywhere possible may not be the best choice. Some common problems with just the lighting upgrade section are people rely on skewed information or poor understanding. Any led fixture is not the right answer because one that may have a higher up-front cost may have a shorter ROI and greater savings in the long run. Contractors will often request alternates to the specified fixtures to save money, or worse, simply buy less expensive ones that look the same, and reduce your overall savings. Motion sensors are not cheap, and when you include installation labor, the ROI may be never for that closet or small room.

One of Humes examples in Force of Nature speaks about how Walmart could not recycle their chicken meat boxes because they were wax lined to prevent leakage. Trying to solve this problem so they could recycle the boxes for money instead of paying to haul them away led to the question of why was the wax needed since each package was now individually shrink-wrapped by the producer? They called the supplier to ask why the chicken was still shipped in wax-lined boxes? The simple answer was because however many years ago you requested wax-lined boxes and never told us otherwise.

United Parcel Service (UPS) did a study that showed never turning left, even if it extends the distance, saves on fuel. They claim it saves them 10 million gallons of fuel, reduces carbon dioxide emissions by 20,000 tons, and allows 350,000 more packages to be delivered per year.

A student field experiment proved replacing an old refrigerator in a break room at a company would save enough in utilities (along with available rebates) to recoup the initial cost in under two years.

Those examples not only show the possible benefits of sustainability programs, they also show how trying to solve one issue can lead to another issue, along with the importance of customer and supplier communication. The point is, implementing lean or sustainable programs can reduce cost and provide positive CSR reporting all in one step. A change in perception from "planting a tree is a waste of money" to "planting a tree on the east side of the building will reduce cooling cost and provide positive CSR."

I breakdown environmental sustainability into three stages:

1. In stage one there are numerous things you can do right away that should have little to no upfront cost. Things like recycling, going

92

paperless where you can, or carefully evaluating your utility bills. This is called low hanging fruit, because it is easy to find, has zero to negligible cost to implement, and the immediate savings help provide momentum to expand on sustainable efforts.

2. The second stage is looking for sustainable improvements like replacing light fixtures with light emitting diode (led) fixtures or maybe upgrading heating, ventilation, air conditioning (HVAC) units, production equipment, delivery vehicles, and so on with more energy efficient models. Keeping in mind a five and ten-year return ROI criteria. When done properly, lighting should easily fall under a five-year ROI with a 10 to 15-year lifespan before major repair or replacement.

3. The third stage is solely for companies looking for a return that is not justifiable in monetary terms; the return is based on positive CSR. This is for companies trying to achieve zero environmental impact. Zero environmental impact is one of those impossible goals that can provide impossible results, but there is a tipping point where the cost will never have a measurable (because positive public perception is not easily measured) monetary return on the investment.

One reason organizations fail to take advantage of these savings is due to their budgeting structure. If utilities are not part of a departments budget, then why would they care about reducing the cost of utilities? If the expense to reduce energy consumption comes out of your budget (light fixtures), but the utility savings are credited to a different budget, why would you do it? You wouldn't.

Manufacturing and installing motion sensors is a huge business sector based on turning off a light switch. We turn the lights on so we can see, but we have no incentive to turn them off. People will start thinking about numerous ways to reduce utility cost (including turning off the lights manually) because they, or at least their supervisor, are incentivized through budgetary constraints.

Many companies set aside a separate budget for sustainability improvements. Ideas for improvements are submitted, and their ROI is weighed against other ideas to determine where the money set aside will be spent. Some companies simply fund this budget each year based on what they can afford, and some fund it by transferring the savings (or a percentage of) created back into the budget. Some companies get creative and bundle short-term ROI projects with longer term ROI projects that may not fall under the desired requirements. This allows both or multiple projects to be presented at a reasonable overall return on investment, the only place in this book where I approve of deception.

The reason I stop at a ten-year ROI is that any ROI proposal, outside of certain capital purchases, over ten years is expected to have technology improvements during that period that may make longer-term investments a better option in the future. The realization of utility consumption being a major factor in cost is a relatively new concept and advances in equipment to become more energy efficient are rapidly changing.

The idea of environmentalist being extremist chaining themselves to trees is all but gone (though extremist still exists) in today's business world. Environmentalist are finding ways to grow colored cotton to reduce the expense and toxic waste of dying clothes, proving that bio-energy recovery systems are efficient energy producers (Anheuser Busch provides approximately 8% of their fuel needs through bio-recovery), finding ways to fund solar and wind electricity generation, and thousands of other cost-effective solutions. Believe it or not, some companies looking for solutions to complex lean issues call environmentalists for suggestions.

We have some significant global pollution issues like removing the plastic and trash from our oceans. I suggest taking a look at the Huffington Post article "The Oceans Are Drowning In Plastic — And No One's Paying Attention" by Dominique Mosbergen. The pictures within this article say more than I ever could. While figuring out how to cost-effectively remove plastic from the ocean without harming ocean life would make a person or company ridiculously wealthy, figuring out how to create or use products that simply do not add to the problem can increase revenue and positive CSR.

These are the reasons I argue the triple bottom line thought process, people and planet are as important to profit today as product. Environmental sustainability and corporate social responsibility are just other avenues to accomplish lean and reduce our expenses with the bonus of positive public perception.

Chapter 7

Six Sigma, One of Many

Every company needs to have a formal project management process in place. A formal set of steps for making company decisions or finding solutions to various issues. Profiteers and educators have manipulated these processes so much overtime to claim something "new" that the origins of many have been written out of history. You may have heard about one of these project management processes called Six Sigma. This is a fine method for the bulk of what I am talking about, but there are other equally useful methods (that use all of the same tools) like A3, PMBOK, Agile, and the good old PDCA (Plan, Do, Check, Act), among others.

Six Sigma is popular because it works and has the greatest amount of marketing. But when you look at Six Sigma, or any other project management process, there is not much there. The Six Sigma methodology is not a revolutionary way of thinking, and it does not provide a radically new set of quality tools. But the success of implementation at Motorola and GE along with the inclusion of Japanese style belt rankings to imply training qualifications has helped launch it into one of today's flavors of the month.

Before I further discuss Six Sigma, I want to discuss these belt ranking accreditations. There are typically five belts, Master Black Belt, Black Belt,

Green Belt, Yellow Belt, and the lesser used White Belt. They are meant to describe the complexity of projects or position within projects someone should be working on. And only higher belts can train people for the lower belts. The issue comes in with regulation; there is none. Someone can take years to learn the steps and available tools to eventually receive their Master Black Belt from a well-trained Master Black Belt at GE Corporation, or online for $600.00. Out of curiosity, I obtained my White Belt certification for free in about 10 minutes online. Agile and Scrum certifications appear to have some of the same issues.

Proponents of Six Sigma try to link it to historical figures like the statistical mathematician Gaussian, or inventor Eli Whitney, this is simply a far-reaching embellishment. So, what is Six Sigma? It is a management process derived from the Total Quality Management (TQM) process to help the Motorola Company reduce manufacturing defects. Motorola trade marked the process (Though I am unsure why since they do not seem to ever enforce it) and used capital letters for Six Sigma in the application. So, we spell Six Sigma with capital letters. The name Six Sigma was chosen due to the mathematical meaning of the sixth standard deviation of a bell curve equating to 99.99966%. Six Sigma is a project management method with the goal of achieving a 99.99966% defect free production rate.

Six Sigma has two standard variations today, DMAIC and DMADV, though I have seen alterations to those acronyms from companies trying to make the process fit their needs.

DMAIC – Improving an existing process - Design, Measure, Analyze, Improve, Control

DMADV – Developing a new product, service, or process - Define, Measure, Analyze, Design, Verify

And that is it, that is the total sum of Six Sigma. You may be saying hey, wait a minute, what about all these other tools mentioned earlier like Kanban, Poke-Yoke, Kaizen, 5S, and so on? Those are individually developed tools that can be used on their own or with any other process like PDCA or PMBOK. They were not conceived specifically for Six Sigma and do not require Six Sigma to be implemented.

On the next page is a chart comparing the various project management methods.

Method	Project Phases								
PDCA	Plan				Do			Check	Act
PMBOK	Initiating	Definition & Planning			Launch & Execution			Monitor & Control	Close
6 Sigma	Define		Measure		Analyze		Improve	Control	
A3	Reason for Action	Initial State	Goal State	Gap Analysis	Solution Approach	Rapid Experiments	Completion Plan	Confirmed State	Insights

As you can see, they are all attempting to achieve the same goal. As simple as PDCA or as Complex as A3 is a preference for what suits your needs. You could use more than one, one for office procedures and one for manufacturing procedures. The key is sticking with the pattern, do not switch back and forth.

Once again, the point of this book is not to reinvent the wheel. Existing project management methods are more than adequate to tell your teams the process of accomplishing a task requires a set of painfully obvious steps. And numerous people have already been trained in accomplishing these steps. The goal of this chapter is to point out that these methods are not independent, exclusive, or complete solutions. We need a process that standardizes our procedures and defines what we will consider as reasonable accountability for the cost of the projects and their implementation. You should start considering these options immediately if you do not already use one or the other. If you already use A system that has certification levels, I would take a quick look at where your people's certifications came from. You additionally need to realize that it is not hard for a potential hire with other certifications like scrum to comprehend Six Sigma processes or visa versa.

Besides the action steps listed above in the project management process steps, there is a reporting method created by Toyota called A3 reporting. All information should be on one side of one sheet of A3 (legal) paper. That's correct, everything you submit for reporting purposes should fit on one side of one sheet of paper or limited to a printable one side of one sheet of A3 paper even if it is never printed. Yes, I understand that there will be numerous things that are hundreds or thousands of pages long, but your report on those thousands of pages WILL fit on one side of one sheet of A3 paper.

Your yearly financial report to the CEO, one side of one sheet of A3 paper. They may ask for a further breakdown of each section that will be submitted on one side of one sheet of A3 paper, but do not think that you are now going to submit one sheet for every category at the beginning. You are going to submit the entire report on one side of one sheet until asked for specifics. And that one page better portray a complete picture. Otherwise, you are doing it wrong.

The reasoning here is that the people you are reporting to are not going to read a 400-page document, though I am sure that there are people who do. If you paint a complete picture on a one-page document, they can ask for any relevant supporting documentation needed. Information that you will be happy to compile onto another single sheet of information. But the need to request additional information could indicate that your original document was lacking.

One Toyota based book states that employee procedures are posted at every stage of production at Toyota. There is an A3 sized paper listing everything that should be done at that station, and it is posted facing away from the employee because it is not there for the employee, it is for management. This way management can easily see what is supposed to be going on at that workstation to better understand the process.

Most people refer to A3 reporting for its use as a problem-solving tool, but this is only one of the many functions available to us. Let's just say that all reports, directions, forms, and anything else used regularly for internal purposes should be limited to A3 paper. I know, I know, you are thinking that this is an unproductive impossibility. All I can say is, Toyota has been doing it for decades, you will figure it out. Information on A3 reporting is widely available on the internet, so we do not need to waste time on the how here.

This chapter is fairly short; the commonality of the available methods does not warrant pages and pages of description. I mean really, they are only process steps to ensure your teams think (plan) about what they want to do, test (do) their plan, make sure (check) the plan works, and then implement (act) their plan. The variations simply expand on the details of each step to create something "new."

Chapter 8

FIT or Fail

The term culture has many ambiguous definitions. What we are talking about here is how the company treats its employees, customers, suppliers, stockholders, community, and humanity in general. Toyota promotes long-term thinking over short-term goals as one of their ingredients for success, and I would have to agree.

I do not believe that this ideal of long-term planning should take pages of explanation to be agreed with. Finding information on the company's trying to save a dollar today and having it put them out of business or costing extraordinary sums of money tomorrow is astoundingly easy. Additionally, we need to understand that sometimes short-term goals keep the doors open now. The idea here is to ensure the short-term goals of today do not result in the need to close the doors next week, year, or decade.

Most of the major problems arise due to the main objectives of investors and many employee bonus structures. Investors are primarily concerned with their return on investment and gauge your success on what they earn this year compared to other investment opportunities. The reasonable plea's from CEO's to ask for a lower investor return this year to invest funds internally or slow production to make changes for future growth are a very hard sale. And bonuses reliant on annual profit margin targets achieved by any means, far too often result in short term cost cutting measures that result in long term damage.

The FIT method is a purely educated hypothesis structured around preventing excessive risk while still allowing calculated risk to be acceptable if justified through long term company benefit expectations. If company leadership and training predispose us to follow industry norms, there needs to be a reasonably justifiable way to allow forward thinkers to step outside of the risk-averse investor expectations without being chopped off at the knees.

If we implement a core business philosophy with a specific set of expectations, then the end results can only have one of two outcomes. Not the outcomes of success or failure, because sometimes the best, logical, and thoroughly thought out ideas fail. We are looking for the outcomes of compliance or noncompliance of procedure.

We must implement ideals that focus solely on the long-term survival of the company. Investors will understand our direction, and we will understand providing positive results for the investors is a major function of long-term survival.

Future – All decisions should be based on their possible long-term impact on the company, stockholders, employees, environment, product, and community.

From this point on every business decision made should be accompanied by a long-term impact statement. Yes, this may seem like an additional step and more paperwork, but it is the first step in justifying decisions that may result in unintended consequences. If you and others within your organization agree certain risks are justifiable for the future of the company, then the risk is justified. If there is no reasonable justification of long-term benefit, then the risk is not justified.

Our second goal is basically common sense. Why would we do anything that would be a detriment to any part of our organization or stakeholders?

Improvement – All decisions and actions should show an improvement to the company, stockholders, employees, environment, product, or community.

If you take a minute to think about it, why would we do anything that doesn't create an improvement in at least one of those areas? If you will notice, the word "actions" was included, this is to include a measurable standard for behavior and working environment.

While every decision does not have to show improvement to every area listed, a detriment to any area should indicate a problem. In the case of employee behavior and the working environment, the actions of others may not always be an improvement, but they should never be a detriment. If there is low employee morale, friction, abuse, and so on, then there is an area that needs to be improved or a detriment that needs to be removed.

Next, we are going to address the more complicated matter of Trust. Trust takes a little bit of clarification. Merriam Webster defines trust as - Assured reliance on the character, ability, strength, or truth of someone or something. One in which confidence is placed.

Since the publication of several books from former Toyota employee's, people have been linking the Japanese culture as a guideline for success. The

107

Japanese rely on their country culture based on honor, but what if your current country of operation does not have those same beliefs? What are you supposed to do, force thousands of years of cultural belief upon your employees? Besides, Japanese companies have a hard time replicating Toyota's success themselves.

Now seems to be a good time to point out that it appears (depending on what list you look at) Toyota has fallen from the number one auto manufacturer spot. Volkswagen has bumped them down to second or third depending on the criteria used. Should we start looking at the VW German culture as the new flavor of the month? Think about it, honor, dedication, and any other positive behavior is something either based on or forms trust.

All around this big green and blue ball we live on, understanding the concept of TRUST is as universal as love, hate, hunger, and so on. We do not need extensive training on how to understand if we trust someone or an organization in general. Though I may need cultural training to understand other cultures better to earn trust, I still understand what I am trying to accomplish. In other words, we are trying to achieve a consensus of emotion that all people understand even if their languages and cultures are different.

I found my cultural anthropology class to be one of the most important and eye-opening experiences of my life. I believe all universities should make cultural anthropology a required course for business majors. People from one end of a state to the other end have variations in behavior and expectations, now imagine Canada to India. Not that there are some opposite sides of the spectrum between Canada and India, they are just different cultures. Several large companies hire an anthropologist to better understand their customers and employees both locally and outside their home country. While the idea of trust is universal, outside of profit and loss just about nothing else business is.

Trust – Every decision or action should be made to instill trust in the company, employees, stockholders, community, and product.

Now do not mistake this line of thought as blind trust. For our purposes, or maybe any purpose, trust needs clear expectations from both parties. You will need to create a clear and concise list of expectations that flows in both directions, what you expect and what others should expect from you. Once created and delivered there should be no confusion or grey area.

Examples would be:

- Your customers can trust that your product or service quality will never be reduced. In other words, the next one they buy will be at least as good as the previous one.
- You trust that your customers will pay on time. You need to provide clear payment expectations at the time of sale.
- You trust that employees will make every effort to provide complete and accurate details of the information they report on. But you need to ensure that they are trained on how to provide what you expect.
- The community trusts that you will not do anything that risks their health. So, don't.

The basics are simple, decide what you want from your employees, train them to understand and have the skills to complete those expectations, and trust them to do their jobs until they indicate you can't trust them. Then apply the process in both up and downstream directions, state what you expect and provide the tools to accomplish those expectations. And the final step is to determine what others expect from you and ensure that happens.

Of course, people may try to manipulate these ideals, but putting them in more detail will not change those people.

Future, Improvement, and Trust (FIT). Do you have a FIT company?

More Examples:

Customers should trust your product. But they do not necessarily need to trust that your product is the best quality. I try to avoid it, but I sometimes buy low-cost tools from those freight stores. I understand that they are a low-quality tool due to the price point, but I do trust that they will work for a preconceived amount of time in a perceived way based on that price. Customers need to trust your company and products are what you say they are, or trust that the second one that they buy will be of the same quality as the first one.

Employees need to have trust in the company. This needs little explaining because you know what would make you trust or distrust anyone else. For instance, layoffs are sometimes needed, your employees should trust that you will do everything in your power to prevent them and if unavoidable, the reason is not poor management or selfish short-term goals.

You should also be able to trust in your employees. This is more complex than trusting not to steal or slack off on the clock. This should mean you trust them to take care of equipment, voice improvement ideas, make certain decisions, or fully comprehend what they are talking about. If a manager comes to you and states that there is a problem but does not have a complete understanding of what that problem is, they have diminished your trust in them to be an effective manager. If an employee fails to point out problems then you lose trust in their dedication.

I could expand on each topic until the end of time, but you should get the idea and understand that the amount of trust is up to you and your implementation of resources to meet expectations. The higher the trust on all levels the greater the results.

Here is an example of a company statement.

"XYZ company and its employees will ensure that all decisions and actions are based on trust, improvement, and the long-term future of the company, stockholders, employees, community, and environment."

Sometimes companies must reduce stockholder payouts, lay off employees, stop doing business with customers, or make decisions that would not necessarily benefit the community or environment to continue operations. We must have flexibility within our inflexible ideals to meet our primary goal of profit, but that flexibility should not diminish long-term goals.

You should understand trust is the most valuable tool for sales, employee relations, investor relations, and public relations in any language or culture. If you implement a policy that guarantees trust in all areas, we do not need to stress honor, dedication, morality, transparency, and so on because they are already there.

To clarify, every major decision should be able to document an expected Future, Improvement, and Trust impact from implementation. And every minor decision should be able to state FIT reasoning for implementation if asked.

Each FIT category impacts the other two categories in some way. I am sure that someone could conceive a scenario where an improvement only impacts the future but not trust or some such combination. Then good for you, pat yourself on the back, enter NONE for that section, and move on (but you are probably doing it wrong). Do you trust them and do they trust you? Is it an improvement or a waste of money? Will it have a positive long-term impact? What is the possible negative impact if something goes wrong?

As with most things in the business world, someone will interpret this to mean every decision should be made by submitting this in written form. Using FIT in written form for everything would only result in a quagmire of paperwork and progress grinding to a halt. While every decision should be made by mentally addressing these topics, only significant decisions above minimal risk should document these steps.

Every project should additionally be accompanied by S.M.A.R.T goals.

S – Specific – What are you doing and how will you know it is done.

M – Measurable – How will you know it meets expectations.

A – Achievable – Can we do it and meet our measurable goals?

R – Relevant – Should we do it? This will be answered in your FIT analysis.

T – Time – When should it be done. A specific time when completion should be expected.

Besides the obvious direction following the FIT philosophy takes us, there is a secondary benefit of justifying progressive projects that involve above average risk. If a questionable idea is assessed through the FIT and SMART steps, then an educated consensus of acceptance or rejection can be made. While this does not guarantee success, failure is justified.

1. An idea is formed and the risk level assessed.
2. Future company impact is evaluated. Both positive and possible negative impacts are documented.
3. The expected areas of improvement are reasoned and documented along with any foreseeable areas of detriment.
4. Any Trust issues are documented.
5. SMART goals are outlined
6. Cost of implementation is assessed
7. Pier or supervisor review, the more the better.
8. The decision to implement or deny.

If these steps are followed with due diligence, then failure is an unforeseen, unintended event without fault. While this will in no way guarantee the safety of the decision maker, it should prove that the decision was made with sound reason and forethought. What more could any investor, board member, or supervisor ask of a leader?

Chapter 9

Cipher Accounting

Cipher – A communication that cannot be understood without knowing the translation key. Or Zero.

Business is not much more than a secret code we are trying to decipher, and our primary objective is to maximize profit by having zero expense. Other goals we look to achieve in our pursuit of long-term profit are zero waste, zero backorders, zero defects, zero environmental impact, and so on. Science fiction? Fantasy? Unrealistic? Maybe. What if we made this paragraph a serious goal? What is the worst that could happen?

I would agree that yes, an actual zero result in expenses is impossible, but there is a tremendous amount of documentation that shows impossible goals often result in previously perceived impossible results and eliminate the "good enough" mentality. So Yes, the cipher method will be focusing on and expecting major strides towards the zero results mentioned above.

The Cipher Method uses the concepts discussed in this book with Cipher Accounting as the primary metric to gauge company overall health and goal results. This chapter is going to be one of those major changes to "the way we have always done it." Currently, your organization relies on existing financial accounting methods for government and stockholder reporting. This type of accounting is misleading and unproductive for improvement. Sure, you will still use financial accounting for legal reasons and investor reporting, but we are going to use Cipher Accounting practices to support the Cipher Method.

Unfortunately, this will cause you to have two sets of accounting records and procedures. The Cipher Method requires and relies on this alternative accounting method to find waste. Traditional accountants may disagree with it, and your traditional accounting methods may show a loss when there is actually significant gain or the other way around.

One example would be where finished goods in inventory are a positive line item under assets in financial accounting, in Cipher accounting finished goods in inventory are a negative because they remain a cost until sold. Like the real world where assumed and projected income does not exist until there is money in your account.

The Cipher Accounting method is very similar to what people are starting to call lean accounting, but there are differences. Where lean accounting uses value added and non-value added, Cipher uses direct cost and indirect cost. Yes, there are other differences besides the words. The intention of Cipher accounting is to show the actual cost to make something or provide a service, the related indirect cost associated with making that product or service, and how any changes to any area will change those costs. In other words, how big picture items like adding or removing a product will change the cost of all other products, or how small items like the accounting department using a bottled water service changes product cost.

The line of thought here is that your company exists to sell a product, so every cost including existence itself is a product cost. If you look at it as a single product company, every single expenditure is what it costs to provide that single product. For some reason, we tend to muddle this reality when multiple products are produced and start talking about unavoidable expenses as something that simply is and doesn't need to be assigned to anything specific. Can you imagine looking at your company and understanding how every cent spent relates to the true cost of manufacturing your products or providing your services? You will start to quickly realize that everything from waste disposal to square footage has an impact on your real product costs.

Here is an example: Let us say that your Product A uses 1/4 of your available production floor space, and Product B uses ½ of your available floor space. You are left with ¼ of your floor space unused, and that space has a cost for rent, lighting, HVAC, and maintenance. The unused area's cost must be absorbed by Products A&B. If you add a 3rd product that uses the remaining available floor space, this cost is removed from products A & B.

You can even expand upon the above example to compare the profit per square foot between product A & B. Does the product that takes up half your available floor space make twice as much as the one taking up 25% of your floor space? While this may not be a reason to throw out either production, it gives you more information to make decisions.

Let's go back to the finished goods in inventory. Traditional accounting shows these goods as an asset, and Cipher accounting shows them as a cost until sold. Cipher accounting views these items as they really are, money sitting

117

on a shelf that may be sold one day or not. Finished goods are not only money sitting on a shelf, but they are also money taking up space that has a cost itself. Cipher accounting is far more detailed and should show you the true cost of everything; estimating is frowned upon unless necessary. Look at it like this; everything is a cost until it is sold. Or in simple terms, profit is measured by money in the bank, not money that could be or may be in the bank at some point.

Direct Cost – Funds spent to make, sell, and store the product. To determine if a line item is a direct cost it must fall under one of two criteria.

1. **The product or service will not exist without the cost.**
2. **The cost would not exist without the product or service.**

Think of it this way, if we stopped making the product right now and pushed every associated piece of equipment, raw material, and finished goods outside, what or who could we get rid of and how much unused space would we have? If we fired someone right now or stopped buying this or that right now could we still make the product?

The cost to light your factory would exist without the product, but the product needs light to be created or exist. This means that only the cost to light the area where the product is created is a direct cost, and the rest of the lighting is an indirect cost unless it can be applied to the direct cost of another product or service.

The same process is used for all employees. If the accounting, maintenance person, or CEO spends 10% of their time working on product A and 30%

working on product B then 10 and 30% of their wages would be applied to each product as a direct cost with the remaining 60% applied as a general indirect cost that will be divided between the two products based on square footage. I used a large number for indirect cost in this example to emphasize the waste we will see in the numbers, why is there so much indirect labor being applied? What are these people doing 60% of the time? Or why does product B require 20% more support labor than product A?

Storage is a direct cost because in a perfect world production material would be used as it arrived and finished product would ship as soon as it was finished. When looking at things like material it is easy to allocate the cost as a direct cost to a product, but what about the labor, equipment, and storage to handle the material? Your shipping and receiving labor is not just a cost of doing business and it is not just a cost to be divided evenly among the number of products you offer as a direct cost. We need to figure out what the actual labor cost is for each product and what the total idle time may be.

You may be asking what the point of this is? We want to see what each product really cost and how each department will affect that cost. We want to see how adding or removing a product line will impact all product cost. We will prove through accounting that the efforts to reduce cost in every area benefits each product or how added cost will do the opposite. We will be able to look at line items for waste and ask why? We want realistic information!

The details of Cipher accounting could be a book itself, but I am trying to not wander that far into the weeds. I am simply providing enough information for a basic understanding to start the process. The main question will be, how do we allocate every expense in an understandable way to every product or service we deliver?

Only cash in is counted as revenue, similar to cash accounting methods. Sales on account are not revenue until paid; building equity is not anything until sold; other equity and depreciation accounts are simply not a factor. The amount of revenue generated is equal to the increase in cash on hand for the period. No more complicated than that.

Before we begin with our accounting of expense, we need to determine our square footage footprint for each product, department, and common area (cafeterias, lobby, parking lot, green space, etc.) that you own or pay rent for. You need to be exact, the accounting department may be on floor three, but they may only use 2/3 of the floor to perform their needed tasks. This would result in 1/3 of floor 3 being allocated to unused space, not accounting. And areas like parking lots can be assigned their own line item, so when we are reviewing indirect cost we will understand what we are looking at and evaluate it appropriately.

I had originally made several charts and graphs to explain the basics of Cipher accounting but the reality of it is any accountant can make a chart of accounts. This method simply relies on a tremendously larger amount of accounts and far more detailed allocation of expenses. Copy paper is not just an office supply expense, it is an office supply expense tracked between departments, positions, and people if done correctly. Labor is tracked in in the minute detail of lawyers hourly billing.

Utilities like electric would work in a similar way. If you do not have submetering in place, you could estimate and make use of your square footage calculations. Estimating utilities is very inefficient, you can track and meter everything in your company down to the receptacle or water faucet if you wanted to. It is all about the question of cost vs benefit of detail. You will at times have no better option than to rely on your square footage calculations to apply certain expenses correctly, like Insurance, rent, subcontracted cleaning services, and so on.

All of your expenses are going to be directed towards each product you offer in the form of either a direct expense or indirect expense. While direct expense is easy to apply to each product, all indirect cost will need to be directed to a single pool. Anything you are unable to apply as a direct cost from the original bill should be directed to an appropriate department expense first. For example, your utility bill would have the direct expense portion based on the description above, but the rest of the bill needs to be applied to departments like accounting, sales, parking, and so on first.

Then for each department the indirect expense can be further evaluated. If accounting spends 10% of their time dealing directly with product A then 10% of the departments total indirect expense can be sent directly to product A's direct expense. Any unapplied expenses for the department will be sent to a single pooled unapplied unallocated expense column for all departments.

By this point, all of your expenses should either be applied as a direct cost for each product or applied to an unapplied unallocated expense pool. Now you need to appropriately apply the unallocated expenses as an indirect cost to each product. While admittedly not perfect, the way we accomplish this is based on the previously determined square footage used by each product. Add your total estimated square foot footprint for each product and then figure the percentage of that total used by each product. Now you will simply apply that percentage of the unapplied unallocated expense pool to the indirect cost of each product.

Now 100% of your total expenses are applied to either the direct or indirect cost of each product provided. Obviously, totaling these two numbers for each product will give you the total cost to produce each product. This number can be used to determine cost per square foot or price per part, etc.

Your monthly deposits should have been divided up in a similar way to apply with each product to find profit per product, part, square foot etc. Tax rebates, depreciation, and other financial accounting focal points only exist if they generate a deposit to be applied, otherwise they lowered a bill paid. Why the bill was lower does not impact our expense application, but is still reflected in the end by being a lower expense or added revenue applied at some point.

The thought of distributing by using product volume, sales revenue, or projected income all have serious flaws that I am not going to spend large amounts of time explaining. Let us just say pushing expense towards high volume products that most likely have a small profit margin to start with or trying to hide it in large margin products does not serve our purpose. Hiding these expenses is not our objective; properly evaluating them is.

Corporate cost for multiple facilities will be spread across all products regardless of location. All of this accomplishes multiple purposes, mostly a true understanding of our cost per product and a place to start asking why. The real key is to quickly understand where waste is hiding, what each product genuinely cost, and how we can best utilize our resources.

Where do the legal fees and related cost of product lawsuits get applied to? When McDonald's was famously sued for having too hot coffee, where did that expense get applied? I have no answer to that question, but I would assume that it was not quality control or coffee expense itself. If we take a minute to think about it, lawsuits that derive from our products or services are in reality a defect cost. When we win a lawsuit, it is a cost of doing business and sent to indirect product cost, when we lose it is a quality control issue with a specific product, hiring policy, training, or management segment and should be reflected in that products direct cost.

For the most part Cipher Accounting is a tool to gain perspective and root cause analysis — a perfect place to use the 5 Why's.

You should now be able to easily see where waste is taking place or what would happen if any specific product or service was removed from or added to the equation. You will be able to enter proposed cost and see how it will relate to the bottom line of all products. Easily detect fluctuations and find the source. And best of all, it creates competition between departments to reduce their own cost.

A CEO should be able to easily follow product cost or indirect cost back to the source and ask why? If GE corporation would have done this to realize their top-heavy structure made any profitable product a loser in the end, they may have not plummeted so far.

I have spoken about the goal of zero to reach the maximum profit, in a perfect system, we would sell, produce, deliver, and collect all at the same time with zero inventory at the end of the day. Our profit should be the maximum amount possible without any environmental impact. So how do we accomplish this impossible goal? I have no idea, but I do know we can't start without understanding what we currently have and what we need to correct.

Common Errors:

Management being allocated as a product direct expense. Unless a manager is the direct report for the people producing, they are an indirect expense. If a manager is twice removed from the actual process you need to start evaluating what part of their pay is a direct expense, if any. What do they actually do that would prevent the product from being created in their absence? Approving payroll or other things is not a direct expense, processing payroll is.

Supply chain personnel visiting suppliers or researching lean processes is not a direct expense, physically ordering raw materials or implementing production changes first hand (You are at least on the floor supervising a production line change you implemented) is. Supply chain savings realizes it self in other areas of reduced cost.

Being in charge of something does not equate to being a direct cost for it. Working to improve the process or reduce expenses does not equate to being a direct cost of creating it, your results will speak for themselves by lowering product expenses. And being an indirect cost does not equate to being irrelevant to production.

Manipulating the numbers to provide some imagined benefit will negatively impact the entire process and be easily discovered with minimal investigation.

Chapter 10

Humility

This is another short chapter, but I believe the importance of the topic deserves its own focal point.

The primary consultant is a person who specializes in the Cipher Method and ensures you are taking the most productive steps towards being a zero waste maximum profit company. A specialty consultant is one that specializes in specific processes or "tools" and should only be brought in at the primary consultant's request.

Changing your methods and people's historical understanding can be very complex and at times confusing. Why should you proceed blindly and waste time reinventing the wheel when you do not need to? I believe the cost of a third party consultant far outweighs the cost of the missteps many take while trying to convert to a lean company.

Have you ever heard of the term desensitize? Mostly we hear it when people are talking about the desensitization of people's morals or values when exposed to violence or other sensitive issues. You are dealing with your facilities, customers, and employees every day and have become desensitized to your surroundings, even if you think otherwise. You know how it is when you open the pantry looking for something and can't find it, then someone walks over and points to it right in front of your face? This is one of many reasons for the Primary Consultant. The current lean production practices may refer to this individual as a sensei.

I quickly learned as a student doing field work, offering help to find waste in a company's existing system is usually met with hostility. People believe that you are questioning their ability to do their jobs correctly or fear that their position could be in jeopardy if you did find something they have overlooked. A primary consultant is adept in diminishing these perspectives that prevent advancement.

Besides being able to see opportunities for improvement that you may overlook on a daily basis, consultants bring with them experience from working with many other companies that may have already experimented with the same processes or had similar issues. One of the most costly and common failures of a company implementing this type of change is they are incorrect about their primary issues. This incorrect focus often results in a company wasting time and money on the wrong things or too many things at once. These errors eventually result in giving up on the entire process due to a lack of measurable results. A primary consultant helps prevent this and overspending in general.

Spending large sums of money to reduce cost is a last resort based on math, not the first step based on hope.

What is the role of the Primary Consultant?

- Inspect your entire company or facility to familiarize themselves with the current situation. They will generally ask for large amounts of available data to assess the situation themselves. They will not become an expert in what you produce or the service you provide. The primary consultant only needs to know enough about your product to make informed decisions on how things are produced or services are delivered.

- Ensure that you are correctly implementing the basic steps outlined in this book and implement expected completion dates for the first phase of these projects. Or recommend specialty consultants be brought in to start the next phase of these projects.

- Evaluate your Cipher Accounting results. Or instruct on the Cipher Accounting process.

- Meet with senior staff to discuss any labor issues or hiring needs and evaluate their thoughts and goals. The consultant will then inform the senior staff of what is needed to move forward.

- Collect data on management processes and company culture.

- A plan will be made to start collecting data on various items. Examples would be spaghetti charts and process flow diagrams.

- At least one main project outside of the basic steps will be initiated with a firm deadline for completion. Main projects could be as complex as rearranging your entire production line.

- Give direction on how to accomplish tasks.

This initial visit may take a day, week, or month depending on your complexity or need. The primary consultant must be from a third party and NOT your employee; the primary consultant is not a full-time onsite position.

The primary consultant will leave after assessment of progression and assigning tasks to be completed by their return. Their job is to teach your employees how to accomplish goals and look for improvements on their own while ensuring that the big picture is on track.

When I say teach, I am not talking about explaining one plus one equals two. I mean telling your people they will need to learn math because figuring out production variances requires math and here is why production variances matter. So, learn math and go find all your production variances by the time I return in 30 days.

Primary consultants are also immune to the problematic employee-employer relationship that may prevent good ideas from being realized. Please keep in mind that a good consultant is not going to be concerned about fitting into your company's culture, only that you have one. Most consultants are notoriously blunt and only care that you are producing results even if they must raise their voice or cause friction to do it.

A company like General Electric would still have one third-party primary consultant that would delegate the tasks out to his or GE's employees as needed. One Cipher Method requirement is that a primary consultant cannot spend more than 30 out of every 90 days at the same facility. Their unfamiliarity with your facility is one of the reasons they are there in the first place, intimacy reduces their effectiveness.

If you are an existing lean company, then you should know how to manage projects and accurately calculate the estimated return on investment for budgeting purposes. Otherwise, your consultant will state if you are ready to start or resume implementing 5 or 10 year ROI projects.

Things that you should NOT do before speaking with the primary consultant:

- Announce to the employees that you are going to initiate this process. Change scares people, and this change needs to be appropriately managed.
- Hire employees to help with this transition. Everything can start with the people you already have.
- Spend money on renovations, new equipment, software, or machinery.

You should also come to terms with the level of authority you will grant the Primary consultant. More authority equates to faster results. If they constantly need to ask permission to speak with people or pause your processes for teaching or improvement ideas, then your results will be slower.

What to look for in a Primary Consultant. They are a Cipher Method approved consultant, or at the very least have a proven track record of lean and sustainability consulting. The Cipher Method is new and people specifically trained to have a complete understanding of this process is limited. Fortunately, lean consultants can guide you in the lean, environmental sustainability, and similar accounting methods mentioned in this book.

Be very wary of consultants that specialize in specific areas like Six Sigma, Kanban, and so on. Not that these consultants can't be good primary consultants, I additionally specialize in energy management. You find that people tend to stick with what they know and unintentionally have you focusing on the wrong spot. If their website and track history seem to focus on specific methods or tools, then you are at your own risk.

To clarify, the reasoning behind the requirement for a third-party consultant is:

- Full-time employees can become desensitized to the environment and overlook waste.
- Full-time employees are more likely to prioritize their career over pushing waste reduction efforts that may seem risky, costly, or disruptive.
- Third party consultants understand the big picture and will not be pressured by managements opinion of priorities.
- Employees more readily accept that studies are being done in their areas due to the pressure from a third party, they are not being singled out and results are not a personal attack on their ability.
- Third party recommendations are generally made with supporting evidence or experience and are taken more seriously than internal recommendations.
- Third party consultants have other customers and care about their reputations more than making waves. If they are a "yes man" that does not push you then their results will be lackluster along with your reviews of their ability.

While most people tend to scoff at the idea of a third-party consultant poking around their kingdom looking for improvements that feel more like criticism of their ability, we must keep in mind that their sole goal is the benefit of the company. These third-party consultants are risk balancers, notice I did not say risk limiters. The opinions of the third-party consultants may encourage senior management to take more risk than normal or prevent them from excessive risk. These consultants are additionally the senior managements qualified second opinion safety net for projects that fail due to unforeseen circumstances or a deciding factor in board acceptance/denial of implementation and funding.

Another function of a third-party consultant is to ensure senior management is functioning as intended by the board and investors. During a third-party evaluation, issues that may be overlooked or obscured by senior management could be revealed. Does meeting expectations equate to maximum profit possible? Or is meeting expectations a result of cut and slash tactics that will cause long term damage? Is the company being run by outdated management practices with handpicked executives to ensure compliance and prevent competition? Is your management standing in its own way to greater success? This is why many investment companies hire primary consultants to thoroughly evaluate their investments.

A Primary Consultant is there to help navigate you through all of the speed bumps while keeping your eye on the destination. This Woodrow Wilson saying is on my business card,

"I not only use all of the brains that I have, but all that I can borrow."

Chapter 11

Cipher Method

By this point, you should have an understanding of what we make or the service we provide is essentially irrelevant to the subject matter. Our function is to ensure we operate and create products or services at the highest quality of our market segment at the lowest possible cost without creating a negative impact to the environment or society. And do those things at an acceptable profit margin.

I brought up the three types of leaders so you could think about the differences between them as you read through these chapters. One of the obvious differences is type I and II leaders have more control over the situation and any risk taken is primarily with their own money or personal reputation. Type III leaders are confined within limits set by investors and boards. The first two types have the goals of personal success gauged by company success, and the third type has the goal of approval gauged by predefined annual profit goals.

The question is how do we create type III leaders that achieve type I and II results within the restrictions of investor and board driven expectations? One issue to overcome is the fear of replacement. Type I and II leaders want managers who can lead and replace them, while type III leaders say they want independent leaders but fear that these go getters may replace them or rock the boat by shining a light on existing inefficiencies.

We need to figure out how to eliminate roadblocks imposed on us by investors. Investors set an expectation, then company executives strive to meet that expectation at any cost. Making these expectations a primary focus limits us in many ways, though ignoring them all together could get you unemployed. A balance between investor expectations, risk, and long-term goals needs to be worked out. If you must do anything to meet a 5% profit increase, some will scavenge every cent they can out of quality and future goals to meet those expectations today and worry about the repercussions next year. Others may simply stop advancing efforts when the goal is reached.

This is where we need to accept impossible goals provide the maximum output for everyone. If your investors demand a 6% increase it should not be on your radar because you are shooting for 25%. If you need to reduce cost by 4% and set that as a department goal, you are doing it wrong because we want to reduce cost by 100%. Your end results should be the maximum possible regardless of meeting that 6% investor goal or not. Then you review the people who made little change and evaluate their ability. Maybe they are operating at maximum quality at the lowest expense possible, but they must prove it. Always setting reasonable goals is not how excelling works.

A very basic description of complex processes to guide us through the chaos of human self-interest. No one size fits all solutions through identical replication of process steps or fancy computer software that understands the human element better than humans. And no promises of seeking or encouraging a specific type of behavior will result in increased long-term profit.

Logic leads us to the understanding managers and employees must reach a mutualistic relationship, and this relationship will lead to the control of output and expenses. You should now grasp how innovation, lean, and sustainability are improved through knowledge, math, and imagination. All employees from the bottom to the most senior position have a strategic thinking value that is foolish to dismiss or ignore. Communication is the key to everything and planning for the future ensures success today.

To help ensure management has an incentive to behave as expected, we need to base success on the accomplishments of their direct reports, lean cost reduction measures, quality of output over quantity, adherence to the Company Conduct Agreement, and dedication to FIT goals. This along with Cipher Accounting oversight will encourage and force type three leaders to behave similarly to type one and two leaders through an acceptable risk barrier to control and improve their budgetary responsibility.

I have spent a fair amount of time speaking negatively about using identical procedures and software to be like everyone else. The problem is not the procedures or software itself, it is the way they are used. Programs like Oracle or Workday are handy tools that can do many things, but this does not equate to doing all things better than qualified humans. They are tools that can make us more efficient if used properly or make us less efficient if the human factor is completely replaced by generalized programmer assumption and limited ability. Maybe some features of that software are of great benefit, but others

137

touted as cost saving features create diminished results that you end up relying on because it is easier.

Education has limits, for universities to educate people on the best way to do something requires a consensus on the best-perceived process steps that result in an erroneous one size fits all format. Financial accounting, physics, statistics, and most math-based studies have little room for interpretation and can churn out students like a photocopier. When we think of classes like business management or entrepreneurial studies, the study material is presented as fact instead of the wide-ranging probability and manipulation of legal and psychology studies. There are no A + B = C solutions to be a successful entrepreneur or manager.

While it sounds simple, to be better than your competition you can't be equal to your competition, achieving it is far more complex. Are your people following the same process steps or philosophy as their people? Is your equal pay to the competition resulting in equally skilled hires? Are your identical software solutions and procedures providing equal results? Is the quantity of employees required to do and manage equal to your competitors? Is your product price, quality, and delivery time equal to your competitors? Now think about where equal is going to get you, nowhere. But do not equate this paragraph to being completely different for the sake of being different is better.

People do the same as others or formalize process steps because it works better than whatever was done before. The key is not blindly accepting it as the best option for you as is. The software may benefit you greatly but using it or any other standardized process can result in a complacency that prevents innovation. Look at those processes drilled into students, software programs used by everyone, and procedures established years ago to see if they are really providing the best output possible.

It is impossible to tell you that if you set up your production line in this way it will provide the maximum benefit for everyone in every situation; or if you always take these procedural steps it will guarantee you the maximum output. We need to understand the folly of these and psychological concepts trying to guarantee anything.

Your company culture was created by management using existing employees. They did not fire everyone and hire all new people to fit within a desired framework. A goal was set and enforced resulting in employee conformance to the new guidelines of acceptable behavior. Hire based on skill and ability, they will conform to your culture or stick out like a sore thumb. You can apply this line of thought to every aspect of your company, the secret is effective enforcement and employee skill. Don't just say you want the shortest lead times or customer satisfaction ratings, provide the tools needed and make it happen.

We need to take a hard look at cost effective solutions to determine if they are actually long term effective. The most economical hiring process may result in below average hires, less expensive material may generate lower quality product, the least expensive tools or equipment could result in extended downtime or increased replacement. Who is running your company? Someone who is only concerned with reducing expenditures for short-term results? Or someone who understands reasoned spending can reduce cost and increase profit on a long-term basis?

Utilize impossible goals and expect impossible results. Push continuous improvement and never settle for good enough. Embrace the cost savings and public relations potential in environmental sustainability. Understand lean and the potential of an effective supply chain division. Realize that you get out of hiring practices what you put into them. And waste can be obscured or misinterpreted in typical financial accounting.

You need to change your perspective on what achievement really is, meeting a predefined goal or eliminating all waste in your system? Are you saving a dollar for the sake of saving a dollar, or ensuring every dollar invested will achieve the maximum return? Only you and your people can answer these questions because every company is unique. Just like people.

Hell, we can barely achieve similar outcomes from different facilities within our own company. How can anyone believe software or scholarly writing is simply going to guide us through the chaos by clicking buttons or following predefined universal process steps ensuring positive results? It is 100% up to you to evaluate your needs and apply the proper tools effectively.

It doesn't matter if you are in the auto, health care, manufacturing, construction, food, weapons, or toy industries, the direction to achieve the majority market share is in this book. If you are a not for profit or government entity the direction towards providing the best service for the least cost is in this book.

The Cipher Method

1. Hire the best employees available based on skill and ability. Understand the differences in education and certificate issuing entities. Learn to balance education and experience. Pay within the industry average pay range. Ensure your software is working with you and not for you. Leave all of the psychology-based reasoning for the end of the hiring process. Use talent to find talent.

2. Utilize 100% of your available intellectual assets. The only people without good ideas are the ones who don't listen.

3. Make employees feel invested in the company through an effective Company Conduct Agreement.

4. Encourage employee and manager communication through efficient and regular reviews.

5. Base promotion and bonuses on quality and direct report success.

6. Train employees to be independent and provide expected results.

7. Utilize lean tools and environmentally sustainable initiatives to reduce cost without reducing quality.

8. Utilize project management tools to control intellectual asset direction.

9. Utilize A3 reporting

10. Ensure management support of the process and utilize change managers.

11. Utilize third-party consultants to counteract desensitization and help ensure the proper implementation of all processes and overall direction.

12. Ensure a FIT culture for long term growth and stability.

13. Make Continuous Improvement a way of life.

14. Lead by example and ensure it is in a way you would expect to be managed and respected.

15. Efficiently communicate both internally and externally.

16. Collect and retain all process, procedure, research, and proposed data.

17. Use Cipher Accounting to find waste, gauge progress, and encourage further improvement.

18. Adequately train to control your cost, quality, and output by ensuring expected behaviors and expected results.

19. Understand that the way everyone does it may make you like everyone else.

20. Good enough equals failure.

The contents of this book are an educated hypothesis based on a single study plus my personal experience and research. I did not delve into the specifics of many topics because every company is different and numerous other books along with internet search engines help us find existing and adequate specifics on those topics.

We can achieve anything; our only boundaries are physics, regulation, imagination, and financing.

I welcome debate based on empirical data, mathematical proof, or multiple identical studies. I will be the first to admit I am incorrect or misguided if the evidence is sound and ecstatic about how proving me wrong led to the correct answer. Though none of this was meant to make people think like me, it was to encourage them to think independently and differently than the competition.

Separate yourself from the industry average, the way everyone does it, good enough, and the way we have always done it. Some ability is natural and can never be taught, finding it in others is the true sign of a great leader.

Consider the shorter length of this book an opportunity to have more time to research what tools fit your specific company and read these suggested books.

- The Goal: A Process of Ongoing Improvement, by E. M. Goldratt, et al.
- Force of Nature: "The Unlikely Story of Wal-Mart's Green Revolution" by Edward Humes
- The Machine That Changed The World by James P Womack, et al.

www.davisconway.com

Author Notes

The field of organizational behavior has unregulated research guidelines and poor funding. Lean improvement advances or failures are rarely documented or researched. We are often left with a direction we would like to move towards, but the available information is often flawed, ambiguous, or skewed towards a specific outcome. Or worse, it is successfully accomplished and kept secret for the fear of replication. We waste countless resources discovering the previously discovered.

It is my intention to donate 10% of my profit from this book (more if anyone actually reads it) to fund related research and collect all available relevant data.

I hope to create a reason for definitive research and multiple replication. I hope to create a research data base of both successful and failed lean conversion attempts and process improvements. And I hope to create a consolidated environmental sustainability database.

Appendix & Index

How can I, in good conscience, speak about environmental sustainability and then fill up pages with public information easily found through any search engine? Is adding technical data 1% of us will actually read necessary? Will doing so to increase the thickness of my book make it more relevant? I'll pass, google it or email me.

Index? It is a short book, read it again if you have to.

There, we just saved some trees or computer processing energy.

www.ingramcontent.com/pod-product-compliance
Lightning Source LLC
Chambersburg PA
CBHW021818170526
45157CB00007B/2637